AF601741

Gratitude

Writing this book was not a solitary effort. Along the way, I have been fortunate to have friends, mentors, and trusted advisors who helped steer me in the right direction. Without these people standing beside me, elevating me with their guidance and encouragement, I would not be here. To them, I am deeply and truly thankful.

A lot of thought, time and rewrites went into writing this. Instead of making this pretty I'll just put words on paper.

"Eddie" - Eduardo J. Sanchez - I've never met anyone like this before in my life. He is loud, funny, thoughtful, intelligent, logical, caring and blunt. Every conversation I've had with this man has taught me something new about the world, myself, philosophy, finance, society, mankind and purpose. I admire this man and aspire to be more like him. If you ever have the opportunity to speak with this man, take full advantage of that moment. Thank you Doctor, simply for being a good person, a good teacher and a good friend.

Haleem Ali - This is the man you call when the shit hits the fan. He doesn't panic, lose his temper, or overreact and get emotional in times of stress. He is the human embodiment of reassurance. Whenever I have felt the urge to react based on emotion and impatience instead of pure fact, he has put me in check and given me the guidance to see the best path forward. I don't think you realize how big of a role you've played in many of my recent decisions. Thank you for leading by example and showing me a better way forward.

Mum - You paved the way. You showed me how. You told me I could be whatever I choose to be. But most importantly, you taught me to be strong and to stand for what I believe in—to not follow the crowd and to be my own person. You built the foundation of who I am today.

Contents

Preface

My name is Aries Daijon-Daniel Russell. I want to start this book by letting you know that I'm an idiot. Outside of the situations and subjects I've been directly exposed to I know very little. Despite my ignorance I've been relatively successful in life, having worked in Banking, National Security and Technology.

Due to my sporadic career changes, I've found myself consistently having to learn vast amounts of complex information in very short periods of time, to be able to answer questions from some very important people about some very serious situations. Over time, I grew used to being thrown in at the deep end and being expected to swim.

Not too long ago I started working at an investment bank, on a small team that manages two global trading businesses. Before starting this role, I had zero practical experience in banking or trading, and I knew very little about how banks work or how the economy works, or even what the economy actually is. To put it bluntly, I knew nothing. Or at least I knew 2 things. I knew that I did not know enough and I knew that I wanted to change that.

When I got the phone call and found out I had got the job, it immediately kicked off a chain of events; a plan I made, to give myself the foundational knowledge I would need to succeed in the role. I went online and I put together a list of online self-paced courses that I knew would teach me the basics of the economy, banking, investments, regulation, finance, and business management. I then spent the next four weeks leading up to the start of my new job studying every day; Finishing courses back-to-back. I dedicated most, if not all of my free time, into learning more than a years' worth of information in a matter of weeks.

Now you might be asking, so what did you learn? Well for starters I learnt that a lot of finance, economics, banking and business courses assume that you already know about finance, economics, banking and business, which in some cases almost drove me to pull my hair out trying to understand some of the concepts. Which leads to where I am now: writing this book. I want to make sure no-one else has to experience what I did, I wanted to make a book that would teach the foundations of the economy and banking, but in a way that can be understood by everyone. This book is for you and me, for anyone who, like myself, hasn't studied economics at university, hasn't worked in finance, and hasn't a clue what a central bank does. This book is for us.

Introduction

Central banks are like the economy's steering wheel, helping to keep things on track and running smoothly. They play a crucial role: They make decisions about interest rates and set rules that help control the flow of money, keep prices stable, and influence how many jobs are available. By doing this, they make sure that the economy stays balanced and grows steadily. It's important for everyone, not just finance experts, to know how these decisions impact our daily lives. Let's break it down so it's easy to understand how central banks help manage our economy and why it matters to all of us.

The Purpose of Central Banks

Central banks are key to the functioning of the modern economy. The overarching purpose of the economy is to facilitate business and improve the quality of life and advancement of mankind. This involves ensuring that resources are efficiently allocated, employment opportunities are available, and the general population can enjoy improved living standards. Central banks contribute to this grand objective through several key roles:

Managing Inflation:

By controlling inflation, central banks preserve the purchasing power of money, ensuring that individuals and businesses can plan for the future with greater certainty.

Promoting Economic Growth:

By stimulating economic activity during downturns and restraining it during booms, central banks help smooth out the business cycle, fostering a stable environment for investment and innovation.

Ensuring Employment:

High employment levels are crucial for economic prosperity. Central banks strive to create conditions conducive to job creation, enabling more people to participate in and benefit from the economy.

Stabilizing the Financial System:

Central banks prevent excessive risk-taking by implementing regulatory measures such as setting higher capital requirements and conducting stress tests. These actions help ensure the stability of financial institutions and maintain the trust and confidence necessary for a functioning economy.

Facilitating International Trade and Cooperation:

Central banks coordinate with each other globally to ensure that monetary policies are aligned, fostering stable international trade and financial systems.

The Ultimate Goal: Human Advancement

The ultimate goal of central banks, and indeed of the entire economic system, is to enhance the quality of life for people around the world. This includes:

- **Raising Living Standards:** By ensuring stable prices and promoting economic growth, central banks help increase incomes and reduce poverty.
- **Fostering Innovation and Development:** Stable economic conditions encourage investment in new technologies and infrastructure, driving progress.
- **Supporting Social and Economic Inclusion:** By promoting policies that create jobs and reduce economic disparities, central banks contribute to more equitable and inclusive societies.

Key Concepts Explained

Liquidity: Liquidity refers to how easily assets can be converted into cash without affecting their market price. Assets are resources owned by an individual or entity that have economic value and can provide future benefits. They can be physical, like property and equipment, or financial, like stocks and bonds. For an economy, liquidity means the availability of cash or easily convertible-to-cash assets in the banking system, which allows businesses and consumers to transact smoothly. High liquidity means there's plenty of cash circulating, which can encourage spending and investment.

Inflation: Inflation is the rate at which the general level of prices for goods and services is rising, and subsequently, purchasing power is falling. Central banks aim to control inflation because too much inflation erodes the value of money, while too little inflation can lead to economic stagnation.

Employment: Employment refers to the number of people who have jobs. Central banks aim to maintain a high level of employment by creating economic conditions that encourage job creation. This means monitoring and adjusting economic growth to ensure that as many people as possible can find work.

Bank Runs: A bank run occurs when a large number of depositors withdraw their funds from a bank simultaneously, fearing that the bank will become insolvent. This can lead to the bank's collapse if it doesn't have enough liquid assets to meet the demand. Bank runs are important because they can destabilize the financial system and lead to broader economic crises.

Economic Recession: An economic recession is a significant decline in economic activity spread across the economy, lasting more than a few months. It is typically visible in GDP, real income, employment, industrial production, and wholesale-retail sales. Recessions are important because they lead to job losses, reduced incomes, and lower living standards

The Business Cycle

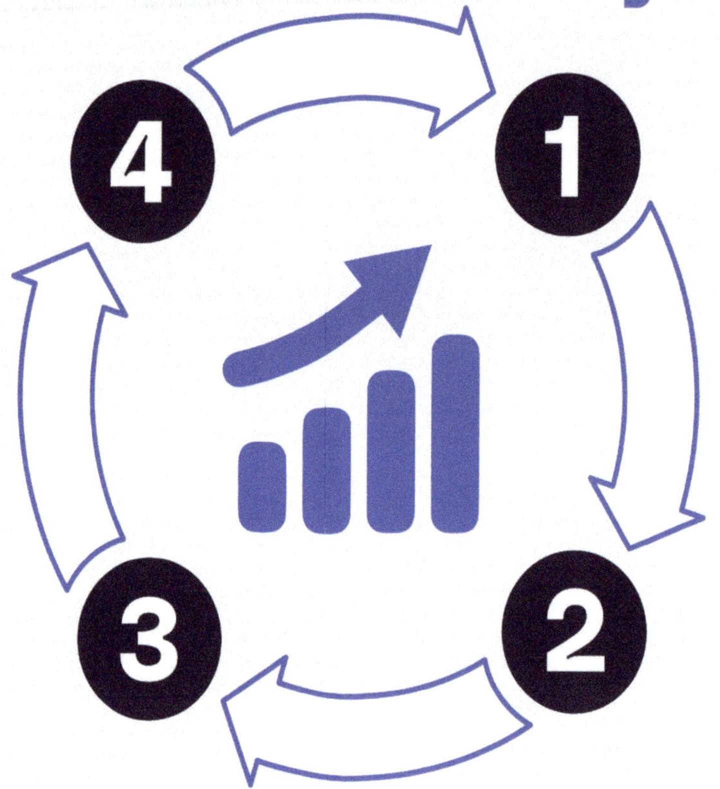

1. Expansion

What Happens

- **Economic Growth:** The economy grows as businesses produce more goods and services.
- **Job Creation:** More people get jobs as companies hire to meet increased demand.
- **Consumer Spending:** Consumers spend more money because they feel confident about their finances.
- **Investment Increases:** Businesses and individuals invest more in new projects, real estate, and the stock market.

Causes

- **Increased Demand:** Higher consumer and business spending boosts production. For example, a new factory opens in town, creating jobs and increasing local spending.
- **Low Interest Rates:** Central banks may lower interest rates to make borrowing cheaper, encouraging spending and investment.
- **Technological Advances:** Innovations can lead to increased productivity and new markets.
- **Government Policies:** Tax cuts and/or increased government spending, can stimulate economic growth. For instance, a government-funded infrastructure project may start, employing local workers and boosting the economy.

Duration

Expansion phases can last several years, typically ranging from 3 to 10 years.

Example

Imagine your local town during an expansion phase. A new tech company sets up a regional office, creating hundreds of jobs. The increased employment leads to higher consumer spending, which attracts more businesses to open, creating a cycle of growth and prosperity.

2. Peak

What Happens

- **Maximum Growth:** The economy reaches its highest point of growth.
- **Full Employment:** Most people who want jobs have them.
- **High Production:** Businesses are producing at full capacity.
- **Inflation Concerns:** Prices may start to rise too quickly due to high demand.

Causes

- **Overheating Economy:** High demand can lead to inflation as businesses can't keep up with consumer spending.
- **Resource Constraints:** Limited availability of labour and materials can push prices up.
- **Central Bank Actions:** To prevent runaway inflation, central banks might raise interest rates, making borrowing more expensive.

Duration

The peak phase is typically short, lasting a few months to a year.

Example

At the peak, every store in your town is busy, everyone seems to have a job, and businesses are doing very well. However, prices for goods and services might start to rise because of the high demand and limited supply. The central bank might raise interest rates to cool off the economy.

3. Contraction

What Happens:

- **Economic Slowdown:** The economy starts to slow down.
- **Rising Unemployment:** People may lose their jobs as businesses cut back on production.
- **Decreased Spending:** Consumers and businesses spend less money.
- **Investment Decline:** Investments decrease as confidence wanes.

Causes:

- **High Interest Rates:** Central banks may raise interest rates to control inflation, making borrowing more expensive and slowing down spending.
- **Reduced Demand:** High prices and borrowing costs can lead to reduced consumer and business spending.
- **External Shocks:** Events like oil price spikes, natural disasters, or geopolitical tensions can disrupt economic activity.

Duration:

Contraction phases, also known as recessions, typically last from 6 months to 2 years.

Example:

In your town, you might notice some stores closing down, fewer job openings, and people being more careful with their money. This could happen because interest rates increased, making loans and credit more expensive, which leads to reduced spending and investment.

4. Trough

What Happens:

- Lowest Economic Point: The economy hits its lowest point.
- High Unemployment: Unemployment reaches its peak.
- Minimal Production: Business production is at its lowest.
- Stabilization Begins: The economy starts to stabilize, setting the stage for recovery.

Causes:

- Reduced Inventories: Businesses deplete their excess inventories and begin to see opportunities for new production.
- Policy Interventions: Central banks and governments may implement policies to stimulate growth, such as lowering interest rates or increasing public spending.
- Consumer and Business Confidence: Gradually, confidence returns as the worst of the downturn passes.

Duration:

The trough phase can be short, lasting a few months to over a year, as the economy begins to recover.

Example:

During the trough, your town feels the effects the most. Many people are out of work, few new businesses open, and everyone is saving money rather than spending it. However, government stimulus programs and lower interest rates might start to take effect, helping to stabilize the economy and prepare it for the next expansion phase.

Why It Matters to You

- Understanding the business cycle is important because it affects everyday life:
- Jobs: Knowing where we are in the cycle can give you insight into job availability.

Why Central Banks Manipulate Interest Rates

Central banks manipulate interest rates to control the economy. The primary objectives are:

Managing Inflation: Keeping inflation in check to maintain the purchasing power of the currency.

Stimulating Economic Growth: Encouraging investment and spending during economic downturns by lowering interest rates.

Ensuring Employment: Striving for high employment by fostering economic conditions conducive to job creation.

Stabilizing the Financial System: Preventing excessive risk-taking and ensuring the stability of the banking system.

Benefits of Central Bank Intervention:

Economic Stability: By controlling inflation and fostering stable economic growth, central banks help maintain a predictable economic environment.

Crisis Management: In times of economic crisis, central banks can provide liquidity and support to prevent financial system collapse.

Confidence Building: Effective central bank policies build confidence among investors, businesses, and consumers, promoting economic activity.

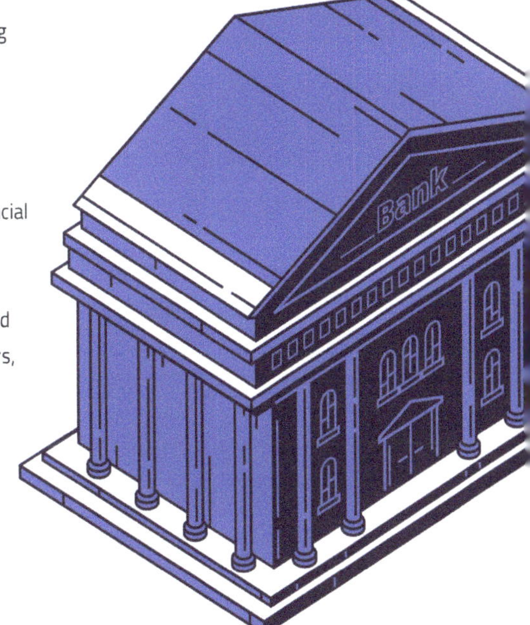

Consequences of Non-Intervention:

Hyperinflation: Without central bank intervention, economies can experience uncontrolled hyperinflation, which can have severe negative impacts. Hyperinflation is an extremely rapid and out-of-control rise in prices, eroding the value of money at an alarming rate. This situation diminishes what people can buy with their income, leading to widespread economic instability. Businesses and individuals struggle to predict future costs, severely impacting financial planning and investment decisions. Those on fixed incomes or with savings see their wealth evaporate, as the purchasing power of their money drastically declines. In extreme cases, the currency can become almost worthless, leading to a collapse in the standard of living and economic chaos.

Deflation: Without central bank intervention, economies can experience uncontrolled deflation, leading to severe negative impacts. Deflation means falling prices, which prompt consumers to delay purchases, expecting even lower prices in the future. This decrease in spending stalls economic activity, causing businesses to earn less, cut jobs, and reduce wages. As the value of money increases, debt becomes harder to repay, adding financial strain. Lower asset values, like homes and stocks, reduce overall wealth and economic stability. Central banks may step in with measures to boost spending and investment to prevent this harmful cycle and maintain economic balance.

Financial Crises: Without central bank intervention, economies are more susceptible to financial crises, which can lead to financial instability, bank runs, and severe economic recessions. Central banks play a crucial role in maintaining confidence in the financial system by acting as lenders of last resort and implementing policies to stabilize markets. As lenders of last resort, central banks provide emergency funding to financial institutions that are struggling to stay solvent. When banks cannot obtain funds from other sources and are at risk of failing, the central bank steps in to lend money, ensuring that the banks can meet their obligations and preventing widespread panic and bank runs. This support helps stabilize the financial system and maintain public confidence in the banking sector. By doing so, central banks help prevent the negative spirals that can lead to deeper economic downturns and ensure that financial markets continue to function smoothly.

Consequences of Non-Intervention

Real world example: Deflation: The Japanese Experience

What Happened

Since the 1990s, Japan has struggled with deflation—a persistent decline in prices. This period, known as the "Lost Decade," saw stagnant economic growth and a prolonged recession.

During Japan's "Lost Decade" of deflation, life became harder for both people and businesses. Prices kept going down, which sounds good at first, but it meant people put off buying things because they expected prices to keep dropping. That led to less money flowing in the economy, which meant businesses made less money and sometimes had to lay off workers. Wages didn't go up much either, so people had less to spend.

For businesses, it was tough because they couldn't raise prices to make more money. Some companies struggled to stay afloat or had to close down. Banks also had problems because people and businesses couldn't pay back loans as easily when their incomes were shrinking.

Where did it all go wrong?

In the late 1980s, Japan saw prices for real estate and stocks soar to incredibly high levels. This was called an "asset bubble." People were buying property and stocks at very high prices because they thought they could sell them later for even more money.

However, this wasn't sustainable because the prices were too inflated compared to what they were really worth. Eventually, the bubble burst, which means the prices suddenly crashed down. This was a big problem because many banks had given out loans based on the high value of these assets. When their value plummeted, people and businesses couldn't repay their loans.

As a result, banks faced a crisis because they had a lot of bad debts they couldn't collect on. This affected the entire economy because banks couldn't lend money as easily anymore, which slowed down economic activity. It also meant people and businesses lost a lot of money because the assets they owned were suddenly worth much less than they paid for them. This whole situation contributed to Japan's economic stagnation throughout the 1990s and beyond, known as the "Lost Decade."

Key Factors Involved

Asset Bubble Burst: In the late 1980s, Japan experienced a massive asset price bubble in real estate and stock markets. When the bubble burst, it led to a banking crisis and a sharp decline in asset prices.

Banking Sector Weakness: Banks were saddled with bad loans, leading to reduced lending and investment.

Insufficient Policy Response: The Bank of Japan was slow to cut interest rates and implement monetary easing, a central bank strategy that increases the money supply to stimulate the economy, often through purchasing government securities and other financial assets from banks and financial institutions to lower borrowing costs and encourage lending.

What Should Have Been Done Differently to Prevent Japan's Deflation Crisis

Cut Interest Rates Quickly

The central bank should have acted more swiftly to lower interest rates. Lower rates make borrowing cheaper, encouraging people and businesses to take loans and spend more. This increased spending can boost economic activity and help prevent a downward spiral of falling prices (deflation). When interest rates are low, consumers are more likely to buy houses, cars, and other goods, and businesses are more likely to invest in new projects, equipment, and hiring.

Recapitalize Banks Early

The government should have injected money into banks earlier to help them recover from bad loans, which could have prevented Japan's deflation crisis. By providing capital to banks, the government can ensure that banks have enough funds to operate and lend to businesses and consumers. When banks are healthy and able to lend, it supports business growth and consumer spending, which are crucial for economic recovery. Recapitalizing banks can also restore confidence in the financial system, encouraging more investment and financial stability. Although this involves the use of taxpayer money, it is an essential step to prevent deeper economic crises, ultimately protecting the broader economy and, in turn, benefiting taxpayers by fostering a quicker recovery and more stable financial environment.

Increase Government Spending

The government could have spent more on public projects like building roads, schools, and hospitals. Such investments create jobs and increase income for workers, who then spend more money on goods and services. This increase in demand can stimulate the economy. Additionally, improved infrastructure can enhance productivity and efficiency in the long run, supporting sustained economic growth.

Provide Direct Payments to Households

Implementing direct payments to families, such as cash payments or tax rebates, could have encouraged more consumer spending even in a deflation scenario. To combat the tendency of consumers to wait for lower prices, the government could have paired these direct payments with temporary incentives to spend. For example, providing limited-time discounts, vouchers, or rebates that expire after a certain period would encourage immediate spending.

A real-world example of this strategy is Japan's "Go To Travel" campaign during the COVID-19 pandemic. The Japanese government offered substantial discounts on travel expenses, including hotel stays and transportation, to stimulate the economy. These discounts were available only for a limited time, which encouraged people to take advantage of the offers promptly rather than delaying their spending.

Support for Innovation and Investment

Offering tax breaks and subsidies for businesses to invest in new technologies and infrastructure could have stimulated economic growth. By reducing the cost of investment, these incentives encourage businesses to expand, innovate, and hire more employees. This not only creates jobs but also enhances the overall competitiveness and productivity of the economy. Supporting innovation can lead to the development of new industries and markets, driving long-term economic stability and growth.

What really happened:

Deflation caused consumers and businesses to delay spending and investment, expecting prices to fall further. This created a vicious cycle of reduced demand, lower production, and job losses. Japan's economy has struggled to achieve consistent growth since.

Key Interest Rates & Financial Instruments and Their Broad Influence

Key Interest Rates & Financial Instruments and their Broad Influence

Fed Funds Rate

The Fed Funds Rate is set by the Federal Reserve in the United States and serves as an important tool in the financial system. This rate influences other key interest rates across the economy and acts as a benchmark for interbank overnight loans. To fully understand the significance of the Fed Funds Rate, it's helpful to first understand what Fed Funds are.

What are Fed Funds?

Fed Funds, or Federal Funds, are reserves held by commercial banks and other financial institutions at regional Federal Reserve banks. These reserves include both required reserves (the minimum amount banks must hold to meet regulatory requirements) and excess reserves (any reserves held above the required minimum). Banks that have surplus reserves (excess reserves) can lend them to other banks that need to meet their reserve requirements. These transactions are typically very short-term, often overnight.

Why Interbank Overnight Loans are Important

Maintaining Reserve Requirements: Banks are required by regulation to hold a certain amount of reserves, which is a portion of their deposits, to ensure they have enough liquidity to meet customer withdrawals and other obligations.

Sometimes, at the end of the day, a bank may find itself with insufficient reserves. To meet the required reserve levels, banks can borrow money from other banks that have excess reserves. These short-term loans are called interbank overnight loans.

Facilitating Smooth Financial Operations

By borrowing and lending reserves among themselves, banks help each other stay compliant with reserve requirements. This ensures that they can continue to provide services like loans and withdrawals smoothly.

Role of the Fed Funds Rate

Cost of Borrowing for Banks: The Fed Funds Rate determines the interest rate at which banks lend to each other overnight. If this rate is low, it becomes cheaper for banks to borrow money to meet their reserve requirements.

This rate is crucial for maintaining liquidity and stability within the banking system.

EFFR Explained: The effective federal funds rate (EFFR) is the interest rate at which US banks lend money to each other overnight. Banks have accounts at the Federal Reserve, and they often need to borrow money from each other to meet daily operational needs. The EFFR is an average of these overnight interest rates, reflecting the cost of borrowing for one night.

Difference Between EFFR and the Fed Funds Rate: The Federal Reserve sets a target range for the federal funds rate, which is the interest rate at which banks lend reserve balances to other banks overnight. The Fed funds rate is a target rate set by the Federal Reserve, intended to influence monetary policy. The EFFR, on the other hand, is the actual rate at which banks conduct these overnight transactions. While the Fed funds rate is a target, the EFFR represents the real-world, market-driven rate, which can fluctuate within the target range set by the Federal Reserve based on supply and demand conditions in the interbank lending market.

Influence on Other Interest Rates

By setting the Fed Funds Rate, the Federal Reserve can indirectly influence interest rates on a variety of loans, including mortgages, car loans, and business loans. Lower rates typically encourage borrowing and spending, while higher rates can help cool off an overheating economy.

Changes in the Fed Funds Rate can ripple through the economy, affecting consumer and business borrowing costs and economic activity.

Economic Stability

By ensuring banks can easily and affordably borrow the money they need to meet reserve requirements, the Fed Funds Rate helps maintain stability in the banking system. This ensures that banks can continue to operate smoothly, which is crucial for the overall health of the economy.

For example, consider a bank that needs an additional $1 million overnight to meet its reserve requirement. If the Fed Funds Rate is set at 2%, the bank can borrow this money at a relatively low cost. If the rate were higher, say 5%, borrowing would be more expensive, and the bank might need to raise interest rates on loans to its customers to cover the higher cost, potentially slowing down economic activity.

The Fed Funds Rate is a vital component in the financial system, ensuring banks have the necessary liquidity to operate efficiently while also influencing the broader economy through its impact on various interest rates. It helps maintain economic stability by affecting the cost of borrowing for banks and, by extension, the rates consumers and businesses face.

Reasons for Its Use

Liquidity Management: Helps banks manage their reserve balances efficiently, ensuring they meet reserve requirements.

Interest Rate Benchmarking: Serves as a reference point for other short-term interest rates, including those for loans, mortgages, and savings accounts.

Monetary Policy Implementation: Used by the Federal Reserve to influence monetary conditions, aiming to control inflation, manage employment levels, and stabilize the economy.

In the Real World: During the 2008 financial crisis, the Fed lowered the Fed Funds Rate to near zero to encourage borrowing and investment, providing liquidity to the banking system and helping to stabilize the economy.

Discount Rate

The discount rate is the interest rate at which the central bank lends short-term money to commercial banks and other depository institutions against government securities. This rate is a critical tool used by central banks to manage liquidity in the banking system and to influence short-term interest rates. By adjusting the discount rate, central banks can either encourage banks to borrow more (by lowering the rate) or less (by raising the rate), thereby impacting the overall money supply and economic activity.

In the United States, the Federal Reserve uses the discount rate as one of its key monetary policy tools, along with the federal funds rate, which is the rate at which banks lend to each other overnight. Although the federal funds rate is not technically a discount rate, it serves a similar purpose by influencing short-term borrowing costs and overall liquidity in the financial system. Other central banks also have their own discount rates, such as the European Central Bank's Marginal Lending Facility rate and the Bank of Japan's Basic Discount Rate. These rates, like the Fed's discount rate, are crucial for managing monetary policy and ensuring the stability of the financial system within their respective economies.

Reasons for Its Use

Short-Term Funding: Financial institutions use the discount rate for short-term borrowing to manage liquidity needs, ensuring they can meet their obligations and continue operations smoothly.

Liquidity Management: Central banks adjust the discount rate to influence the money supply. Lowering the rate encourages borrowing and boosts liquidity, while raising it reduces borrowing and tightens liquidity.

Monetary Policy Implementation: By adjusting the discount rate, central banks influence economic growth and inflation. Lower rates stimulate economic activity, while higher rates can cool down an overheating economy.

In the Real World: The Federal Reserve lowered the discount rate during the 2008 financial crisis to provide liquidity to struggling banks. The European Central Bank used a similar approach during the Eurozone debt crisis to support financial institutions.

By understanding the discount rate and its role in the financial system, one can appreciate how central banks manage liquidity, influence short-term interest rates, and implement monetary policy to promote economic stability and growth.

Overnight Indexed Swap (OIS) Rate

An Overnight Indexed Swap (OIS) is a special type of swap. It's a short-term agreement, often lasting just one day, where two parties exchange interest payments.

What is a Swap?: A swap is a financial agreement between two parties to exchange (or "swap") cash flows or financial instruments, which are assets that can be traded, over a set period. In the context of an OIS, one party pays a fixed interest rate, while the other pays an interest rate based on an overnight index (a benchmark rate for overnight borrowing). Swaps are commonly used for hedging.

Example: Imagine two companies, Company A and Company B. Company A has a loan with a variable interest rate that changes daily, making their interest payments unpredictable. Company B has a loan with a fixed interest rate that doesn't change. To hedge against the risk of unpredictable interest payments, Company A and Company B agree to swap their interest payments. Company A pays Company B a fixed interest rate, while Company B pays Company A the variable interest rate. This way, Company A can better predict its interest expenses, and Company B can take advantage of potential decreases in interest rates.

Hedging Explained: Hedging is like buying insurance. It's a strategy used to offset potential losses in investments by taking an opposite position in a related asset. For instance, if a company is worried that interest rates will go up, it can enter into an OIS to lock in a fixed rate, thus protecting itself from the risk of rising rates. This way, even if interest rates increase, the company will still pay the agreed fixed rate.

How OIS Rates Are Determined: Overnight Index Swap (OIS) rates are determined using a combination of central bank benchmark rates and actual market transactions. Central banks set the underlying benchmark rates that serve as the foundation for OIS rates. These benchmarks include the Effective Federal Funds Rate (EFFR) in the United States, SONIA in the United Kingdom, and €STR in the Eurozone, among others. OIS rates are available for all major currencies, reflecting expectations of future central bank rates.

Financial institutions calculate OIS rates by averaging the interest rates from numerous overnight borrowing transactions between banks. These transactions are then used to derive the daily effective rates, such as the EFFR in the U.S., which serves as the index for the corresponding OIS.

The OIS market is vast, with trillions of dollars in transactions tied to OIS rates. For instance, in the U.S. alone, the notional amount of OIS trades can exceed hundreds of billions of dollars per day. These swaps play a crucial role in interest rate risk management and the broader financial system.

Central Banks and Interest Rates: Central banks, like the Federal Reserve in the U.S., set key interest rates that affect the economy. When the Fed changes its target interest rate (the fed funds rate), it influences the rates that banks charge each other for overnight loans. The OIS rate is based on these overnight rates, so when the central bank changes its rates, the payments in an OIS change too.

Importance of the OIS Rate: The OIS rate is important because it shows what people think central banks will do with interest rates. This information helps businesses and investors make better decisions about borrowing and lending money. It also provides a benchmark for other financial products, meaning it helps set the standard for what interest rates should be.

Reasons for Its Use

Hedging Interest Rate Risk: This is a way to protect against changes in short-term interest rates. It works like a safety net, helping to avoid potential financial losses if interest rates go up or down unexpectedly.

Benchmarking: used as a starting point, or reference, for setting other interest rates in financial contracts.

Market Expectations: Reflects market expectations of future central bank policy actions and economic conditions.

In the Real World: During the transition from LIBOR to SOFR, many financial institutions used OIS rates to manage their exposure to changing interest rates and to benchmark their contracts.

In summary, the OIS rate is a crucial financial tool that helps institutions manage interest rate risk, set benchmarks for other financial contracts, and gauge market expectations of central bank policies. Understanding the OIS rate and its implications can help businesses and investors make informed financial decisions.

Eurodollar Market

Involves U.S. dollars deposited in banks outside the U.S., with rates sensitive to the Fed Funds Rate, directly impacting global borrowing costs.

The Eurodollar market is where U.S. dollars are deposited in banks outside the United States, mainly in Europe. It allows international banks and businesses to lend and borrow U.S. dollars outside of U.S. regulations. This market is large and liquid, providing a critical source of short-term financing and interest rate hedging. Interestingly, there are often more U.S. dollars in the Eurodollar market than within the United States itself, highlighting its significance in global finance.

Interest Rate Hedging Explained: Interest rate hedging is a strategy used to protect against the risk of interest rate changes. It involves using financial instruments, which are assets that can be traded, to stabilize interest payments and costs. For example, if a company is worried that interest rates will increase, it can use a swap to exchange its variable-rate interest payments for fixed-rate payments, thus avoiding the risk of rising rates. This way, even if interest rates increase, the company will still pay the agreed fixed rate, ensuring more predictable financial outcomes.

Example: Imagine a multinational corporation that plans to borrow money to expand its operations. The corporation is concerned that interest rates might increase in the future, making the cost of borrowing more expensive. To hedge against this risk, the corporation enters into a swap agreement where it will pay a fixed interest rate and receive a variable interest rate. This way, if interest rates rise, the corporation's borrowing costs remain predictable and stable, protecting it from the impact of higher rates.

Reasons for Its Use

Global Borrowing and Lending: Used for borrowing and lending U.S. dollars outside the U.S. to take advantage of interest rate differentials.

Interest Rate Arbitrage: Participants engage in arbitrage opportunities due to differences between domestic and Eurodollar interest rates. Arbitrage is the practice of taking advantage of a price difference between two or more markets.

Funding and Investment: Provides a significant source of funding for international trade and investment.

Real-World Example

During the 1980s, the Eurodollar market became a popular source of funding for U.S. companies. These companies found that borrowing U.S. dollars from banks outside the United States, particularly in Europe, offered lower interest rates compared to borrowing within the U.S. This was because the Eurodollar market was highly competitive and not subject to the same regulations as the domestic market.

Example: Take a large U.S. corporation like IBM. Suppose IBM needed to borrow $100 million for expansion but found that domestic interest rates were around 8%. Meanwhile, banks in the Eurodollar market were offering loans at 6%. By borrowing from the Eurodollar market, IBM could save 2% on interest, which amounts to $2 million per year on a $100 million loan. This significant saving made it more feasible for IBM to undertake its expansion plans, demonstrating the practical benefits of the Eurodollar market.

LIBOR to SOFR Transition

LIBOR, or the London Interbank Offered Rate, is an interest rate used globally. It's the rate at which major banks lend to each other for short-term loans. LIBOR is crucial because it serves as a benchmark, which is a reference point, for various financial products like loans and mortgages. It's calculated daily for different currencies and loan durations. LIBOR was traditionally published by the Intercontinental Exchange (ICE) Benchmark Administration.

LIBOR was widely used because it provided a consistent and transparent benchmark for setting interest rates. This made it easier for financial institutions to price loans and financial products, ensuring uniformity across the global markets.

LIBOR faced significant problems due to manipulation scandals. Some banks submitted false interest rates to benefit their trades and appear more stable than they were. This led to legal actions and a loss of trust in LIBOR as a reliable benchmark. The manipulation highlighted flaws in the rate-setting process, which was based on estimates rather than actual transactions.

Due to these issues, regulators decided to phase out LIBOR by the end of 2021 and replace it with a more reliable benchmark.

SOFR, or the Secured Overnight Financing Rate, was chosen to replace LIBOR. SOFR is based on actual transactions in the U.S. Treasury repurchase agreement (repo) market, where banks borrow and lend Treasuries overnight. This makes SOFR a more reliable and accurate benchmark. The Federal Reserve Bank of New York publishes the SOFR rate.

Unlike LIBOR, which was based on estimates, SOFR is based on actual transaction data, making it more transparent and reliable. Because it relies on real transactions, SOFR is less susceptible to manipulation

Reasons for Its Use

Interest Rate Benchmarking: Serve as benchmarks for setting interest rates on various financial products.

Transparency and Reliability: Transition to SOFR aims to enhance the integrity and reliability of interest rate benchmarks used in financial contracts.

Based on Real Transactions: Unlike LIBOR, which was based on estimates, SOFR is based on actual transaction data, making it more transparent and reliable.

Reduced Manipulation Risk: Because it relies on real transactions, SOFR is less susceptible to manipulation.

Prime Rate

The prime rate is the interest rate that banks charge their most creditworthy customers for loans, credit lines, and other forms of credit. It often mirrors the Federal Funds Rate set by the Federal Reserve. It's crucial because it influences borrowing costs across the economy. When the prime rate goes up, borrowing becomes more expensive, affecting everything from mortgages to credit card interest rates. This directly impacts individuals by potentially increasing their loan payments and reducing disposable income. For businesses, higher prime rates mean increased costs for expansion and operations, potentially affecting hiring and investment decisions.

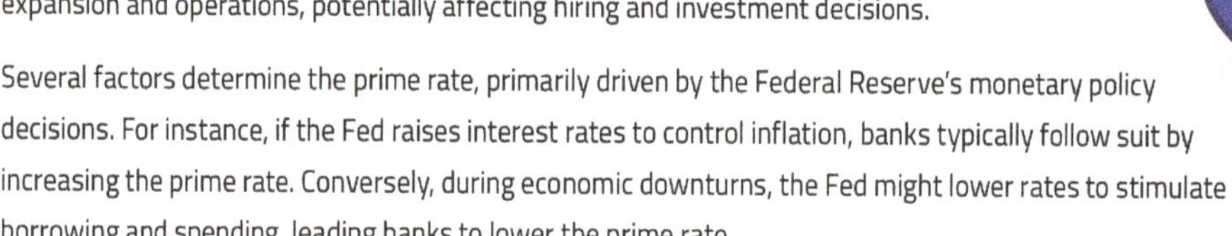

Several factors determine the prime rate, primarily driven by the Federal Reserve's monetary policy decisions. For instance, if the Fed raises interest rates to control inflation, banks typically follow suit by increasing the prime rate. Conversely, during economic downturns, the Fed might lower rates to stimulate borrowing and spending, leading banks to lower the prime rate.

Real-Life Example: During the 2008 financial crisis, the Federal Reserve significantly lowered the Federal Funds Rate to near zero in an effort to stimulate the economy. In response, banks reduced the prime rate, making loans cheaper. This was intended to encourage borrowing and spending by both consumers and businesses to help revive the economy. For instance, mortgage rates fell, making it more affordable for people to buy homes or refinance existing mortgages. Lower interest rates on credit cards and business loans also helped reduce costs for consumers and businesses, providing much-needed relief during the economic downturn.

Reasons for Its Use

Interest Rate Benchmarking: Serves as a benchmark for setting rates on various consumer and business loans.

Credit Risk Pricing: Banks use the prime rate to price loans based on the perceived credit risk of their most creditworthy customers.

In the Real World: During economic downturns, banks often lower the prime rate in line with reductions in the Fed Funds Rate to stimulate borrowing among their most creditworthy customers, as seen during the 2020 COVID-19 pandemic.

Swap Rate

The swap rate is the fixed interest rate one party agrees to pay in exchange for receiving a floating rate, like LIBOR or SOFR, over a set period. This exchange allows parties to manage their exposure to interest rate fluctuations. For instance, a company with a variable rate loan might enter into a swap to pay a fixed rate and receive a floating rate, thereby stabilizing its interest payments. Central banks can influence swap rates by adjusting short-term interest rates and managing the overall availability of money in the economy. This control helps stabilize financial markets and manage economic conditions.

Swaps are most often used for hedging. Hedging is a strategy used to manage or reduce various financial risks, such as price changes, interest rate shifts, or currency fluctuations, by taking an offsetting position or making an investment that balances the potential loss in another.

Difference from the OIS Rate: While both the swap rate and the OIS rate involve exchanges of interest payments, they differ in structure and purpose:

1. **Nature of the Rates**
    - **Swap Rate:** Involves a fixed interest rate exchanged for a floating rate (such as LIBOR or SOFR) over a set period. It is used to hedge against interest rate fluctuations or to speculate on changes in interest rates.
    - **OIS Rate:** Involves exchanging a fixed interest rate for an overnight index rate, often the effective federal funds rate (EFFR). The OIS rate is used primarily as a tool for managing interest rate risk over very short periods, typically overnight.
2. **Underlying Benchmark**
    - **Swap Rate:** The floating rate can be based on various benchmarks like LIBOR or SOFR.
    - **OIS Rate:** Specifically based on the overnight index, which is a benchmark for overnight borrowing rates. The overnight index is calculated based on actual overnight borrowing transactions between banks, reflecting the average rate banks charge each other for overnight loans.
3. **Purpose and Use**
    - **Swap Rate:** Used broadly in the derivatives market for hedging longer-term interest rate risks and for speculative purposes.
    - **OIS Rate:** Used mainly for very short-term interest rate risk management, particularly in the context of managing liquidity and short-term interest rate exposures.

What is a Derivative?: A derivative is a financial contract whose value is based on, or derived from, the value of an underlying asset, index, or rate. Common underlying assets include stocks, bonds, commodities, interest rates, and currencies. Derivatives are used for various purposes, including hedging risks, speculating on price movements, and gaining access to otherwise hard-to-trade assets or markets.

Example of a Derivative: Imagine you own a small bakery, and you need to buy flour every month. You worry that the price of flour might go up in the future, making it more expensive for you to run your business. To protect yourself against this risk, you enter into a derivative contract with a supplier. You agree to buy flour at a fixed price for the next six months. Even if the market price of flour goes up, you will still pay the agreed-upon price, ensuring that your costs remain stable. This contract is a derivative because its value is based on the price of flour.

Role of the Swap Rate in Derivatives: The swap rate plays a critical role in the derivatives market, particularly in interest rate swaps. An interest rate swap is a type of derivative where two parties exchange cash flows based on different interest rates. One party typically pays a fixed rate (the swap rate) while the other pays a floating rate, such as LIBOR or SOFR. This allows both parties to manage their interest rate exposure according to their financial needs and market expectations. For example, a company with a variable rate loan might enter into a swap to pay a fixed rate, thus stabilizing its interest payments and reducing uncertainty. The swap rate, therefore, serves as a key component in these transactions, helping to determine the cost and benefits for the parties involved.

Forward/Futures Rate

Rates agreed upon for financial transactions to be conducted at a future date. These rates are derived from expectations about future interest rates, inflation, and economic conditions.

A forward contract is a private agreement between two parties to buy or sell an asset at a specified price on a future date. For example, an airline might agree to purchase jet fuel from a supplier at $2 per gallon in three months. A futures contract, meanwhile, is similar but traded on an exchange with standardized terms. For instance, a utility company might buy a futures contract for electricity at $50 per megawatt-hour for delivery in six months. Forwards are customizable and carry more risk, while futures are standardized and generally considered safer.

Additionally, forwards are typically settled at the end of the contract term, meaning the physical delivery or cash settlement happens on the contract's expiration date. Futures, on the other hand, are marked to market daily, which means they are adjusted for gains and losses at the end of each trading day, reducing the risk of significant default at the contract's end. Counterparty default risk refers to the risk that one party in the contract will not fulfil their obligations, which is higher in forward contracts due to the lack of daily settlement and standardization seen in futures.

Reasons for Its Use

Hedging Future Risk: Used to hedge against future price or interest rate fluctuations.

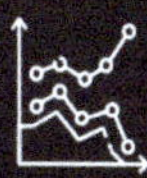

Speculation: Traders use forward and futures contracts to speculate on future movements in prices or interest rates.

Price Discovery: Helps in the discovery of future prices based on current expectations of economic conditions.

In the Real World: Airlines frequently use futures contracts to hedge against future fuel price increases, locking in prices to manage costs and reduce the impact of volatile fuel prices.

How Marked to Market is Calculated:

1. **Daily Settlement Price:** Each day, the exchange sets a settlement price for each futures contract based on the closing price (the last price at which the asset was traded during the trading day) of the asset.
2. **Daily Gains and Losses:** The difference between the contract's original price and the new settlement price determines the gain or loss for the day.
3. **Adjustment of Margins:** These gains and losses are credited or debited to the trader's margin account. A margin account is a type of brokerage account where the broker lends the customer money to buy securities. A broker is a person or firm that acts as an intermediary between buyers and sellers. A margin is the amount of money or equity (the value of the securities minus what you owe to the broker) that the customer needs to contribute as a percentage of the current market value of the securities.
4. **Final Settlement:** At the end of the contract term, the final settlement price is used to determine the total profit or loss for the contract.

Example of Marked to Market: Imagine a cattle farmer named John who enters into a futures contract to sell 100 cattle at $1,200 per head, with delivery set for three months from now. Here's how marked to market works:

1. **Day 1:** John agrees to sell 100 cattle at $1,200 per head. The total value of the contract is $120,000.
   - Initial Margin: John and the buyer each need to post an initial margin, which is a small percentage of the contract's total value as collateral to ensure they can meet their obligations. Let's assume the initial margin requirement is 10% of the contract's value. So, John and the buyer each post $12,000 as collateral.
2. **Day 2:** The market price of cattle goes up to $1,250 per head. The new value of John's contract is $125,000.
   - **Daily Gain/Loss:** John's account is debited with the $5,000 loss, while the buyer's account is credited with a $5,000 gain.
   - **Margin Account Adjustment:** John's margin account is now $7,000 ($12,000 initial margin - $5,000 loss), while the buyer's margin account is $17,000 ($12,000 initial margin + $5,000 gain).
3. **Day 3:** The market price of cattle drops to $1,220 per head. The new value of John's contract is $122,000.
   - Daily Gain/Loss: John's account is credited with a $3,000 gain, while the buyer's account is debited with a $3,000 loss.
   - Margin Account Adjustment: John's margin account is now $10,000 ($7,000 previous balance + $3,000 gain), while the buyer's margin account is $14,000 ($17,000 previous balance - $3,000 loss).

4. **Margin Calls:** If the market price moves significantly against John, causing his margin account to fall below a certain threshold (known as the maintenance margin), he will receive a margin call. A margin call requires John to deposit additional funds into his margin account to bring it back up to the required level. If John fails to meet the margin call, the broker may liquidate his position to cover the losses.
5. **End of the Contract:** This process continues daily until the end of the contract. If the final market price of cattle is $1,230 per head, the final value of John's contract is $123,000. John has made a total profit of $3,000, which is credited to his account.

This daily adjustment process helps ensure that both parties regularly settle their gains and losses, reducing the risk of a significant default when the contract expires. It makes the financial markets more transparent and ensures that the contract values accurately reflect current market conditions.

Relationship to Central Banks: Central banks, such as the Federal Reserve in the United States, play a crucial role in influencing forward and futures rates. They do this through their monetary policy decisions, including setting short-term interest rates and engaging in open market operations. When a central bank raises or lowers interest rates, it directly impacts the cost of borrowing and the returns on savings. This, in turn, affects the expectations about future economic conditions, which are reflected in forward and futures rates.

For example, if a central bank signals that it plans to raise interest rates to combat inflation, forward and futures rates for financial instruments like bonds, currencies, and commodities will adjust to reflect these expectations. Traders and investors will anticipate higher future rates and adjust their positions accordingly. Conversely, If the central bank lowers interest rates to stimulate the economy, forward and futures rates will typically decrease in response to the expectation of lower borrowing costs and increased economic activity.

Central banks' actions and policies are key drivers of forward and futures rates, as these rates reflect market expectations of future economic conditions influenced by central bank decisions. Understanding this relationship helps market participants make informed decisions when entering into forward and futures contracts.

Understanding Interest Rate Swaps

An interest rate swap is a financial agreement between two parties to exchange one stream of interest payments for another, over a set period of time. Here's a simplified explanation to help you understand how it works:

Fixed Rate: One party agrees to pay a fixed interest rate to the other party. This rate stays the same throughout the life of the swap.

Floating Rate: The other party agrees to pay a floating interest rate, which can change over time. This rate is usually tied to a benchmark, like LIBOR or SOFR

Example: Imagine Company A has a loan with a variable interest rate, which means their interest payments can go up or down depending on market rates. They are worried about rates increasing and want more predictability. Company B, on the other hand, has a loan with a fixed rate but believes rates will go down and wants to benefit from potentially lower rates.

Swap Agreement: Company A and Company B enter into a swap agreement. Company A agrees to pay Company B a fixed rate, and in return, Company B agrees to pay Company A a floating rate. Now, Company A's interest payments are predictable, and Company B can benefit if rates go down.

Payments: Each party pays the other based on the agreed rates. For example, if Company A's fixed rate is 3% and Company B's floating rate is based on SOFR + 1%, the payments will be calculated accordingly and exchanged

By swapping interest payments, both companies manage their interest rate risks better according to their expectations and needs.

Other Main Benchmarks

EURIBOR (Euro Interbank Offered Rate): A benchmark rate that reflects the average interest rate at which eurozone banks are willing to lend unsecured funds to other banks in the euro wholesale money market.

SONIA (Sterling Overnight Index Average): A benchmark rate for overnight unsecured transactions in the sterling market. It is based on actual transactions and reflects the average interest rate banks pay to borrow sterling overnight.

TONAR (Tokyo Overnight Average Rate): A Japanese benchmark for overnight unsecured loans. It is based on the weighted average of interest rates of unsecured overnight call transactions.

EONIA (Euro Overnight Index Average): Previously used for overnight lending in the euro area, EONIA has been largely replaced by €STR (Euro Short-Term Rate), which is based on borrowing costs from eurozone banks.

Open Market Operations (OMO)

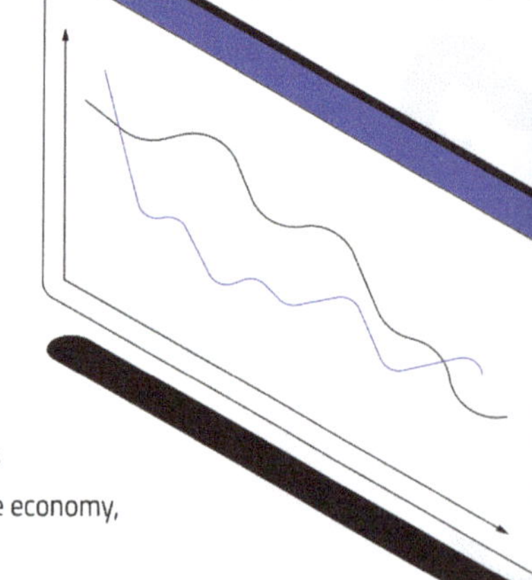

Central banks directly impact the liquidity and interest rates in the economy by buying and selling government bonds, influencing both short-term and long-term rates.

Open market operations help manage a country's money supply and financial stability by buying and selling government bonds, which directly affects liquidity (availability of money) and interest rates. When central banks buy bonds, they inject money into the economy, making it easier and cheaper to borrow, which lowers interest rates. Conversely, selling bonds withdraws money from the economy, making borrowing more expensive and raising interest rates.

For everyday people, lower interest rates mean cheaper loans for things like houses and cars, but also lower returns on savings. Higher interest rates make borrowing more expensive but offer better returns on savings. For businesses, lower interest rates reduce borrowing costs, encouraging investment and expansion, while higher rates can constrain growth by making loans more costly and reducing consumer spending. This dynamic influences overall economic activity, impacting employment, inflation, and economic growth.

Reasons for Its Use

Liquidity Management: Used by central banks to control the amount of money in the banking system.

Interest Rate Control: Influencing the supply of money allows central banks to adjust interest rates to achieve their monetary policy objectives.

Economic Stabilization: Helps stabilize the economy by managing inflation and supporting economic growth.

In the Real World: During the COVID-19 pandemic, the Federal Reserve conducted large-scale open market operations, purchasing substantial amounts of government bonds to inject liquidity into the economy and keep interest rates low.

Real World Example:

In 2018, Turkey experienced a severe currency crisis. The value of the Turkish lira was rapidly decreasing due to a combination of political instability, high inflation, and concerns about the central bank's independence. This decline in the lira's value made it more expensive for Turkey to import goods and led to higher prices for consumers.

To address this crisis, the Central Bank of Turkey used several measures, including open market operations. They started by selling large amounts of foreign currency reserves. Foreign currency reserves are assets held by a central bank in foreign currencies, such as dollars or euros. They are used to back liabilities (debts and obligations) and influence monetary policy.

Liabilities: These are debts or obligations that an entity owes to others. For a central bank, liabilities can include money in circulation and deposits from commercial banks.

Foreign currency reserves help central banks manage these liabilities by providing a buffer of readily available funds. Additionally, by buying or selling these reserves, central banks can influence the exchange rate and stabilize their own currency.

When selling foreign currency reserves wasn't enough to support the lira, the central bank took more aggressive steps by increasing interest rates significantly. In September 2018, the Central Bank of Turkey raised its key interest rate from 17.75% to 24%, a substantial increase aimed at curbing inflation and stabilizing the lira. To put this in perspective, during the same period, the U.S. Federal Reserve's interest rate was around 2%, and the European Central Bank's rate was 0%. This stark difference highlights the extreme measures Turkey had to take compared to more stable economies.

Additionally, the Central Bank of Turkey conducted open market operations by selling government bonds. By selling these bonds, they effectively removed money from circulation. With less money available, borrowing costs increased further, which helped to control inflation and stabilize the currency.

These actions were aimed at reducing the amount of money in the economy to curb inflation and support the lira. While these measures were painful, leading to higher borrowing costs and slowed economic growth, they helped to prevent a complete financial meltdown. The aggressive use of open market operations, alongside other measures, helped to restore some degree of stability to the Turkish financial system and reassured investors.

Regulatory Measures to Control Capital

Reserve Requirements

Central banks set reserve requirements, which are rules that specify the minimum amount of money that banks must keep on hand and not lend out. By adjusting these requirements, central banks can control how much money banks can create through lending.

When reserve requirements are high, banks have less money available to lend. This can make it harder and more expensive for people to get loans for things like houses and cars. For businesses, it means less access to credit for expansion and operations, which can slow down growth.

On the other hand, when reserve requirements are low, banks can lend out more money. This makes it easier and cheaper for people to get loans, which can stimulate spending and investment, helping to boost the economy.

Central banks adjust reserve requirements to help keep the economy stable and growing. During tough economic times or when growth is slow, central banks might lower reserve requirements so banks can lend more money. This encourages people and businesses to borrow and spend more, which helps boost the economy.

However, when the economy is growing too fast or when prices are rising quickly (inflation), central banks might raise reserve requirements. This makes borrowing harder and slows down spending. Controlling borrowing and spending helps to manage inflation, which is when the prices of goods and services increase, reducing people's purchasing power.

Real World Example: Reserve Requirements in India

In 2012, India's economy faced significant challenges, including a slowdown in growth, high inflation, and a lack of liquidity in the banking system. These issues made it difficult for businesses to expand and for people to obtain loans. To address these problems, the Reserve Bank of India (RBI) took several measures, including lowering the cash reserve ratio (CRR).

Economic Slowdown

The economic slowdown in India was caused by multiple factors:

- Global Financial Crisis Aftershocks: The 2008 global financial crisis had lingering effects. Although India initially weathered the crisis better than many other countries, the global economic environment remained weak, affecting India's exports and foreign investments.
- Policy Paralysis: There was a period where the government was slow to implement economic reforms and infrastructure projects. This reduced investor confidence and slowed economic growth.
- High Interest Rates: To combat inflation, the RBI had kept interest rates high, making borrowing more expensive and slowing down investment and consumption.

Reasons for Its Use

Liquidity Management: Ensure that banks maintain sufficient reserves to meet their obligations.

Monetary Control: Adjusting reserve requirements influences the money supply and overall economic activity.

Financial Stability: Adequate reserves help prevent bank runs and enhance the stability of the financial system.

In the Real World: In 2020, the Federal Reserve reduced reserve requirements to zero for all depository institutions, freeing up additional funds for lending to support the economy during the COVID-19 pandemic.

High Inflation

Inflation in India during this period was driven by several factors:

- **Food Prices: Poor monsoon seasons led to lower agricultural yields, pushi**ng up the prices of essential food items.
- Fuel Prices: High global crude oil prices increased the cost of fuel, impacting overall inflation.
- Supply Chain Bottlenecks: Inefficiencies and bottlenecks in the supply chain added to the costs of goods and services, contributing to higher prices.

Lack of Liquidity in Banks

Banks in India faced a liquidity crunch due to:

- High Non-Performing Assets (NPAs): Many banks had a high level of loans that were not being repaid, reducing their ability to lend.
- Tight Monetary Policy: The RBI's high interest rates meant that borrowing was expensive and there was less money circulating in the economy.
- Reduced Foreign Investment: Global uncertainty led to reduced foreign investment inflows, tightening the availability of funds in the banking system.

Challenging Global Economic Environment

The global economic environment also posed challenges:

- Eurozone Crisis: The sovereign debt crisis in the Eurozone led to financial instability in Europe, reducing demand for Indian exports.
- Slow US Recovery: The slow recovery of the US economy from the 2008 financial crisis impacted global trade and investment flows.
- Weak Global Trade: Sluggish global trade growth due to economic uncertainties and protectionist policies affected emerging markets like India.

Measures Taken by the RBI

To address these issues, the RBI implemented several measures:

- Lowering the CRR: The RBI lowered the cash reserve ratio (CRR), which is the percentage of a bank's total deposits that must be kept in reserve and not lent out, from 6% to 4.25%. This allowed banks to have more money available to lend, thereby increasing the availability of credit.
- Interest Rate Cuts: The RBI reduced interest rates to make borrowing cheaper.
- Open Market Operations: The RBI bought government bonds to inject money into the banking system.

Impact and Results

The measures taken by the RBI had several positive effects:

- Increased Lending: Banks had more money to lend, making it easier for businesses to get loans for expansion and for individuals to obtain personal and home loans.
- Stimulated Growth: The increased availability of credit helped stimulate economic activity, leading to a gradual recovery in growth rates.
- Managed Inflation: While inflation remained a concern, the combined measures helped stabilize prices over time.

Overall, the RBI's decision to lower the cash reserve ratio, along with other supportive measures, helped alleviate the economic slowdown, increased the availability of credit, and contributed to stabilizing the Indian economy during a challenging period.

How Central Banks Enforce Reserve Requirements

Central banks enforce reserve requirements through regular monitoring and reporting by banks. Banks must report their reserve levels to the central bank, typically on a daily or weekly basis. If a bank falls below the required reserve level, it may face penalties or be required to borrow funds to meet the shortfall.

Penalties: Central banks may impose financial penalties on banks that fail to meet reserve requirements. These penalties can include fines or additional reserve requirements in the future.

Borrowing: Banks that fall short of their reserve requirements can borrow funds from other banks in the interbank market or from the central bank itself, often at a higher interest rate.

Consequences of Not Having Reserve Requirements

Without reserve requirements, banks might lend out a higher proportion of their deposits, potentially leading to excessive risk-taking and reduced liquidity. This could increase the likelihood of bank runs, where a large number of depositors withdraw their funds simultaneously, leading to bank failures and financial instability.

Consequences of Falling Below Reserve Requirements

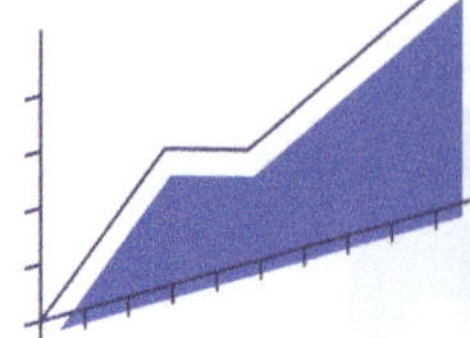

If a bank falls below its reserve requirements, it may face several real-world consequences:

Increased Borrowing Costs: The bank may need to borrow funds at higher interest rates to meet its reserve requirements, increasing its operational costs.

Regulatory Scrutiny: Persistent failure to meet reserve requirements can attract increased scrutiny from regulators, leading to potential sanctions or corrective measures.

Reputation Damage: Falling below reserve requirements can damage a bank's reputation, reducing customer confidence and potentially leading to a loss of deposits.

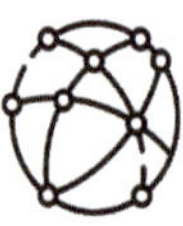

In the Real World: During the 2008 financial crisis, some banks faced severe liquidity issues and struggled to meet reserve requirements. This led to increased borrowing costs, regulatory intervention, and, in some cases, the failure of banks such as Lehman Brothers.

Advanced Monetary Tools

Quantitative Easing (QE)

Quantitative easing is a monetary policy tool used by central banks to help boost the economy when it is struggling. It works by increasing the amount of money in the banking system. Here's a simple way to understand it:

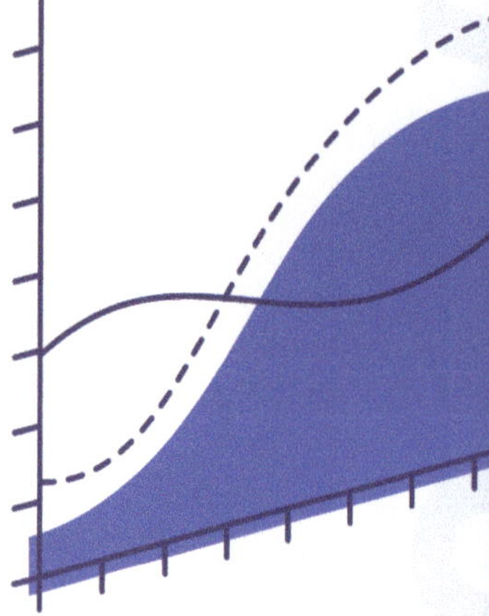

1. **Purchasing Long-Term Securities:** The central bank buys long-term securities, like government bonds, from the market.
2. **Printing Money:** To buy these bonds, the central bank effectively prints new money. The central bank has the ability to create money as and when needed, but this action is not without consequences. This doesn't mean they physically print banknotes; rather, they create money electronically, which increases the total amount of money in the banking system.
3. **Increasing Money Supply:** By purchasing these bonds, the central bank adds more money to the banks' reserves. With more money available, banks have more funds to lend to individuals and businesses.

Reasons for Its Use

Stimulate Economic Activity: By lowering long-term interest rates, QE encourages borrowing and investment

Increase Money Supply: Injecting liquidity into the economy supports lending and spending, boosting economic growth.

Combat Deflation: Helps prevent deflation by encouraging consumption and investment.

In the Real World: During the 2008 financial crisis, the Federal Reserve implemented multiple rounds of QE, purchasing large quantities of government bonds and mortgage-backed securities to inject liquidity into the financial system and lower long-term interest rates.

4. **Lowering Interest Rates:** With more money available to lend, the competition among banks to lend this money increases. This competition drives down interest rates, making it cheaper for people and businesses to borrow money.

5. **Encouraging Borrowing and Spending:** Lower interest rates mean that loans for things like homes, cars, and business investments become more affordable. As people and businesses borrow and spend more, this helps to boost economic activity.

6. **Combating Recessionary Pressures:** During times of economic slowdown or recession, people tend to spend less money, which can make the economic situation worse. Quantitative easing aims to counteract this by encouraging spending and investment, helping to stimulate economic growth.

Example to Illustrate: Imagine a central bank wants to help the economy grow. They decide to use quantitative easing by buying $1 billion worth of government bonds. To do this, they create $1 billion in new money. This new money goes to the banks that sold the bonds. Now, these banks have $1 billion more to lend out. Because they have more money to lend, they lower their interest rates to attract borrowers. With lower interest rates, more people take out loans to buy houses and cars, and businesses borrow to invest in new projects. All this borrowing and spending helps to boost the economy.

However, it's important to note that while central banks can create money when needed, doing so can lead to consequences such as inflation if too much money is created. This is why central banks must carefully balance their actions to avoid causing other economic problems.

In summary, quantitative easing involves the central bank creating new money to buy government bonds, increasing the money supply, lowering interest rates, and encouraging borrowing and spending to stimulate the economy.

Detailed Breakdown of the 2008 Crisis and QE

The crisis began with the bursting of the housing bubble, leading to a high rate of mortgage defaults and the collapse of major financial institutions.

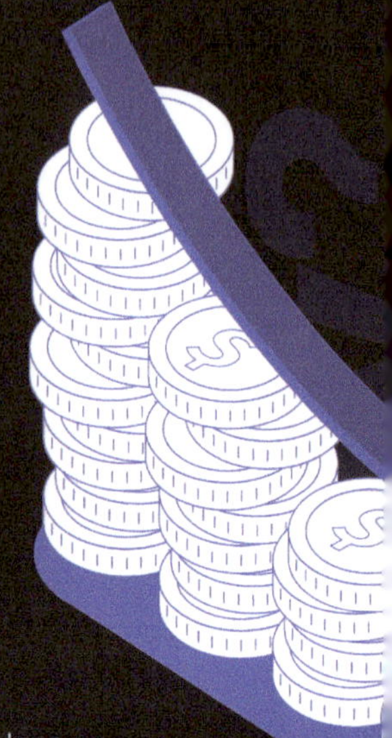

This caused widespread panic in financial markets, as banks and investors faced huge losses. Many people lost their homes and jobs, resulting in a severe economic downturn that affected millions globally. Governments and central banks had to step in with massive bailouts and stimulus packages to stabilize the economy and restore confidence. A direct bailout involves the government providing financial support to struggling companies, often by giving them money to keep them afloat. For example, the U.S. government provided a direct bailout to the insurance giant AIG, giving them $182 billion to prevent their collapse. In addition to direct bailouts, central banks implemented quantitative easing (QE), where they bought financial assets to inject money directly into the economy. This measure aimed to lower interest rates and increase lending to spur economic growth.

Initial Response: The Federal Reserve cut the Fed Funds Rate to near zero to make borrowing cheaper.

First Round of QE (QE1): In late 2008, the Fed started purchasing $600 billion in mortgage-backed securities (MBS) to stabilize the housing market.

Second Round of QE (QE2): In 2010, the Fed purchased $600 billion in long-term Treasury securities to further reduce interest rates and stimulate the economy.

Operation Twist: In 2011, the Fed began selling short-term Treasury securities and buying long-term ones to flatten the yield curve and encourage long-term investment.

Yield Curve Explained: The yield curve is a graph that plots the interest rates of bonds with different maturity dates. Typically, short-term bonds have lower interest rates than long-term bonds. The shape of the yield curve helps investors understand economic expectations. A normal upward-sloping yield curve suggests economic growth, while an inverted yield curve can indicate a potential recession.

Third Round of QE (QE3): In 2012, the Fed launched an open-ended program to purchase $40 billion in MBS per month, later increased to $85 billion, until significant improvement in the labour market was seen.

These measures provided liquidity, lowered borrowing costs, and helped restore confidence in the financial system.

Quantitative Tightening (QT)

Quantitative tightening (QT) is the reverse process of quantitative easing (QE). It is a monetary policy tool used by central banks to reduce the money supply in the economy. This is achieved by selling long-term securities, such as government bonds, back into the market or by allowing these securities to mature.

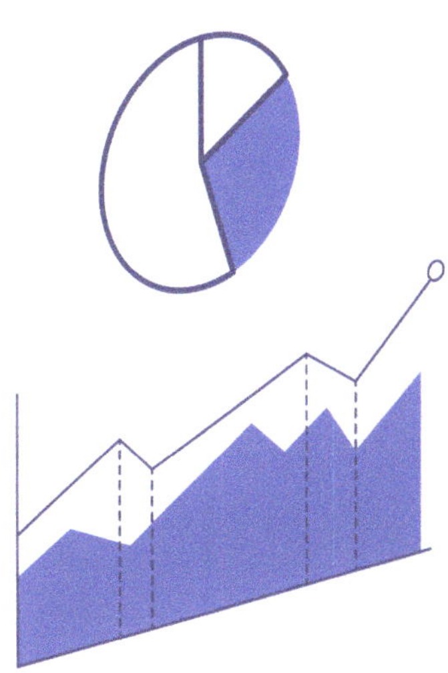

By doing this, the central bank withdraws money from the banking system, leaving banks with less money to lend. As a result, interest rates increase, making borrowing more expensive for individuals and businesses. Higher interest rates discourage borrowing and spending, which helps to cool down economic activity and control inflation.

Essentially, quantitative tightening aims to slow economic growth by raising the cost of borrowing and reducing the amount of money circulating in the economy. This helps counteract inflationary pressures and stabilize the economy.

Reasons for Its Use

Control Inflation: By reducing the money supply, QT helps manage inflationary pressures.

Raise Interest Rates: Selling securities increases interest rates, making borrowing more expensive and cooling down economic activity.

Stabilize Economy: Helps stabilize the economy by preventing overheating and reducing inflation risks.

In the Real World: In 2017, the Federal Reserve began QT by gradually reducing its holdings of government and mortgage-backed securities, aiming to normalize its balance sheet and prevent inflation as the economy recovered.

Real World Example: Quantitative Tightening in Australia

In 2019, the Reserve Bank of Australia (RBA) began implementing quantitative tightening measures after several years of quantitative easing and low interest rates aimed at stimulating the economy. The decision to shift from easing to tightening was based on several factors:

1. **Economic Recovery:** The Australian economy was showing signs of recovery with increased economic growth and improved employment rates. The RBA observed that the measures taken during the quantitative easing phase had effectively supported the economy through the global financial crisis and subsequent years.
2. **Rising Inflation:** With the economy recovering, inflationary pressures began to build up. Prices for goods and services were starting to rise, which indicated that the economy was potentially overheating. The RBA's primary mandate is to maintain price stability, so managing inflation became a key concern.
3. **Sustainable Growth:** The RBA wanted to ensure that economic growth was sustainable and not driven by excessive borrowing and speculative investment. By tightening the monetary policy, the RBA aimed to prevent the formation of asset bubbles and maintain long-term economic stability.

Implementation of Quantitative Tightening

The RBA's approach to quantitative tightening involved allowing its holdings of government bonds to mature without reinvesting the proceeds. This gradual reduction in the balance sheet meant that as bonds reached their maturity dates, the money received from these bonds was not used to purchase new bonds. Instead, it was effectively removed from the financial system.

Here's a more detailed look at how they did this:

1. **Maturing Securities:** The RBA held a significant amount of government bonds and other securities that had been purchased during the quantitative easing phase. As these bonds matured, the RBA chose not to reinvest the proceeds. This natural reduction in the balance sheet helped withdraw liquidity from the market.

2. **No New Purchases:** Unlike during quantitative easing, when the RBA actively purchased new securities to inject money into the economy, during quantitative tightening, no new purchases were made. This ensured that the money supply gradually decreased.

3. **Monitoring Economic Indicators:** Throughout the process, the RBA closely monitored various economic indicators, such as inflation rates, employment figures, and GDP growth. This allowed them to adjust their strategy as needed to ensure that the tightening measures were having the desired effect without causing undue harm to the economy.

The decision to implement quantitative tightening was seen as timely and necessary by the RBA to ensure that inflation remained within their target range and that economic growth was balanced and sustainable. By carefully managing the reduction in the money supply, the RBA aimed to foster a stable economic environment that could support long-term prosperity for Australia.

Forward Guidance

Central banks use this tool to communicate future policy paths, influencing market expectations and economic forecasts, thereby affecting forward and futures rates.

Forward guidance is a communication tool used by central banks to signal their future monetary policy intentions to the public.

By providing information about expected interest rate changes and economic outlooks, it helps influence financial decisions and market expectations. This transparency aims to stabilize the economy by reducing uncertainty about future monetary policy actions.

Reasons for Its Use

Market Stability: Reduces uncertainty about future policy actions, helping stabilize financial markets.

Economic Behaviour: Influences the behaviour of businesses, consumers, and investors based on expected future interest rates and economic conditions

Policy Effectiveness: Enhances the effectiveness of monetary policy by aligning market expectations with central bank objectives.

In the Real World: During the COVID-19 pandemic, the Federal Reserve used forward guidance to signal that interest rates would remain low for an extended period, helping to support economic recovery by reassuring markets and encouraging borrowing and investment.

Understanding Forward Guidance

Purpose: To provide transparency about the future course of monetary policy, helping businesses and investors make informed decisions.

Methods: Central banks may issue statements about future interest rate paths or economic conditions that would warrant policy changes.

Impact: Clear guidance helps reduce market volatility and aligns expectations, which can magnify the effects of monetary policy.

The first known use of forward guidance was by the Bank of Japan in the 1990s. Japan was facing long-term economic problems, so the Bank of Japan started telling the public that they would keep interest rates low for a long time. This was done to encourage people to borrow and spend more money, helping to boost the economy.

Forward guidance became really important during the 2008 financial crisis. At that time, central banks like the Federal Reserve in the United States couldn't lower interest rates any further because they were already near zero. So, the Fed began clearly stating that they would keep rates low for an extended period. This helped reduce uncertainty and encouraged borrowing and spending, which supported the economic recovery.

Economic Crises

Understanding the 2008 Financial Crisis

The 2008 financial crisis, also known as the Global Financial Crisis (GFC), was a severe worldwide economic downturn that began in 2007 and lasted until 2009. It was the most serious financial crisis since the Great Depression (1929). The crisis was primarily triggered by the collapse of the housing bubble in the United States, which had been fuelled by risky lending practices and the proliferation of subprime mortgages.

The Housing Bubble and Subprime Mortgages

- **Housing Bubble:** In the early 2000s, housing prices in the United States began to rise rapidly, creating a bubble. This was driven by high demand for homes, low interest rates, and easy access to credit. For instance, home prices in cities like Las Vegas and Miami skyrocketed, with many homes doubling in value within a few years.

- **Subprime Mortgages:** Banks issued a large number of subprime mortgages, which are loans given to borrowers with poor credit histories. These loans carried higher interest rates due to the increased risk of default. However, many borrowers were unable to keep up with the payments as interest rates rose and housing prices began to fall.

Consider the case of a couple in California who bought a $500,000 home with a subprime mortgage. Initially, their monthly payments were affordable due to a low "teaser" interest rate. But after a couple of years, their interest rate adjusted upwards significantly, causing their monthly payments to double. Unable to afford these payments, they defaulted on their loan.

When such borrowers started defaulting on their loans, it led to a cascade of financial failures. The values of mortgage-backed securities, which are investments based on home loans, plummeted. Financial institutions around the world, which had heavily invested in these securities, faced enormous losses

Understanding Mortgage-Backed Securities (MBS)

- **Mortgage-Backed Securities (MBS):** To understand why the defaults on subprime mortgages had such a massive impact, it's crucial to grasp what mortgage-backed securities are. An MBS is a type of investment that is similar to a bond but is made up of a bundle of home loans bought from the banks that issued them. Investors in an MBS receive periodic payments similar to bond coupon payments.

Here's a step-by-step breakdown of how an MBS works

- **Origination:** A bank issues home loans to borrowers. These loans might be to individuals buying homes in places like Atlanta, Denver, or New York.

- **Bundling:** The bank then sells these loans to a government-sponsored enterprise like Fannie Mae or Freddie Mac, or to an investment bank. These institutions bundle thousands of individual home loans into a single investment product known as a mortgage-backed security.

- **Sale to Investors:** The MBS is sold to investors, such as pension funds, mutual funds, and other financial institutions. Investors receive regular payments derived from the mortgage payments made by homeowners.

- **Example:** Imagine you invest in an MBS. Essentially, you are buying a piece of a pool of mortgages. If the homeowners whose mortgages are in the pool make their payments on time, you receive a portion of those payments as returns on your investment.

The problem arose when homeowners, especially those with subprime mortgages, began defaulting on their loans. The flow of payments to investors in MBS was disrupted, causing the value of these securities to drop dramatically. Financial institutions that held large amounts of MBS faced significant losses, leading to a crisis of confidence and liquidity in the financial markets.

Major Financial Failures

One of the most notable collapses was Lehman Brothers, a major global financial institution. Lehman Brothers filed for bankruptcy in September 2008, which sent shockwaves through the global financial markets. To understand the severity of this collapse, consider that Lehman Brothers was worth over $600 billion in assets just before it filed for bankruptcy. The collapse of such a large institution highlighted the severity of the crisis and led to widespread panic and turmoil in financial markets worldwide.

Real-World Example: Lehman Brothers was a massive investment bank with assets of over $600 billion. Its bankruptcy was the largest in U.S. history and resulted in a loss of thousands of jobs. This event triggered a domino effect, leading to severe declines in the stock markets and a freeze in credit markets globally.

The Federal Reserve's Response

In response to the escalating crisis, the Federal Reserve (the central banking system of the United States) implemented several measures to stabilize the economy:

Lowering Interest Rates

The Federal Reserve cut the Federal Funds Rate, which is the interest rate at which banks lend to each other overnight, to near zero. This move aimed to make borrowing cheaper for banks, businesses, and consumers, thereby stimulating economic activity by encouraging spending and investment.

Real-World Example: By lowering interest rates, a small business owner in Texas was able to refinance their business loan at a much lower rate, reducing monthly payments and freeing up cash to invest in new equipment and hire more staff.

Quantitative Easing (QE)

Quantitative Easing (QE) involved the Federal Reserve purchasing large amounts of government bonds and mortgage-backed securities. By buying these securities, the Fed injected liquidity (money) into the financial system, which helped lower long-term interest rates and encouraged lending and investment. The increased liquidity also aimed to restore confidence in the financial markets.

Real-World Example: A family in Florida, looking to buy their first home, benefited from lower mortgage rates due to QE. This made their home loan more affordable, allowing them to enter the housing market despite the ongoing financial instability.

Lending Facilities

The Federal Reserve established various emergency lending facilities. These programs provided liquidity to banks and other financial institutions to ensure they could continue their operations and avoid collapse. By providing emergency funds, the Fed helped stabilize the financial system and prevent further financial institution failures.

Emergency Lending Facilities Explained: The emergency lending facilities were essentially loans provided to financial institutions facing liquidity crises. These were not free handouts but loans that the institutions were required to pay back, often with interest. The funding for these facilities came from the Federal Reserve's balance sheet, which expanded significantly during the crisis. Here are some key details:

Total Borrowed: During the peak of the crisis, the Federal Reserve's emergency lending programs reached over $1 trillion in outstanding loans.

Who Paid for Them: Ultimately, the cost of these lending facilities was borne by the Federal Reserve, which can create money. However, the goal was for the loans to be repaid by the borrowing institutions. The interest paid on these loans provided income for the Federal Reserve.

Types of Lending Facilities

- **Term Auction Facility (TAF):** TAF was introduced to provide short-term loans to banks. Banks could bid for these loans at auctions, and the collateral requirements were lower than usual to make it easier for banks to access needed funds. Collateral requirements refer to the assets that banks must pledge to secure a loan. Lowering these requirements meant that banks could use a broader range of assets to secure the loans, making it easier for them to borrow money.

- **Primary Dealer Credit Facility (PDCF):** PDCF provided overnight loans to primary dealers (large financial institutions that trade directly with the Federal Reserve). This facility aimed to support the liquidity of these dealers, which are crucial to the functioning of financial markets.

- **Term Asset-Backed Securities Loan Facility (TALF)**: TALF was designed to support the issuance of asset-backed securities (ABS) by providing loans to investors who purchased these securities. ABS are financial products backed by loans, leases, or other receivables, similar to mortgage-backed securities but based on different types of debt. These products are important because they provide liquidity to the market and make it easier for consumers and businesses to get loans. By supporting the issuance of ABS, TALF aimed to increase credit availability to households and small businesses, helping to stimulate economic activity.

- **Commercial Paper Funding Facility (CPFF):** The CPFF was created to provide liquidity to the commercial paper market. Commercial paper is a type of short-term unsecured debt issued by companies to finance their day-to-day operations. "Unsecured" means that the debt is not backed by any collateral. During the crisis, the commercial paper market froze as investors lost confidence. The CPFF allowed the Federal Reserve to purchase commercial paper directly from issuers, ensuring that companies could continue to obtain the short-term funding they needed to operate. This facility was crucial for maintaining the flow of credit to businesses and preventing further economic contraction.

Government Interventions

In addition to the Federal Reserve's actions, the U.S. government took significant steps to address the crisis.

Nationalization of Fannie Mae and Freddie Mac

Fannie Mae (Federal National Mortgage Association) and Freddie Mac (Federal Home Loan Mortgage Corporation) are government-sponsored enterprises (GSEs) that play a crucial role in the U.S. housing market. GSEs are financial services corporations created by Congress to enhance the flow of credit to specific sectors of the economy and to make those segments more efficient and transparent. Fannie Mae and Freddie Mac buy mortgages from lenders and either hold them in their portfolios or package them into mortgage-backed securities. In September 2008, due to severe financial difficulties, both entities were placed into conservatorship by the U.S. government.

Conservatorship Explained: Conservatorship is a legal status wherein an entity (in this case, the government) takes control of a troubled company to stabilize it. The goal is to restore the company to health and return it to private control once it is stable. For Fannie Mae and Freddie Mac, this meant that the government took over their operations to ensure they could continue to function and support the housing market.

Real-World Example: A homeowner in Ohio with a mortgage through Fannie Mae was able to refinance their loan under more favourable terms, thanks to the stability provided by the government's intervention.

Troubled Asset Relief Program (TARP)

The Troubled Asset Relief Program (TARP) was introduced in October 2008. TARP was designed to purchase distressed assets, particularly mortgage-backed securities, from banks. By removing these troubled assets from banks' balance sheets, the program aimed to strengthen the financial sector and restore confidence in the banking system. TARP also included provisions to inject capital directly into banks to ensure they had sufficient funds to operate.

Real-World Example: Bank of America received a significant capital injection through TARP, which helped stabilize the bank and allowed it to continue lending to small businesses and consumers.

Regulatory Reforms

In the aftermath of the crisis, significant regulatory reforms were enacted to prevent a similar crisis from happening again. The Dodd-Frank Wall Street Reform and Consumer Protection Act, passed in 2010, was one of the most notable reforms. This comprehensive legislation aimed to increase transparency and oversight in the financial system, protect consumers, and reduce the risk of future financial crises. Key provisions included the creation of the Consumer Financial Protection Bureau (CFPB) and stricter regulations on financial institutions.

Real-World Example: The Dodd-Frank Act introduced the Volcker Rule, which restricted banks from making certain kinds of speculative investments. This meant that a bank in New York could no longer engage in high-risk trading activities that could endanger the financial system, thus providing greater protection to consumers.

Global Impact of the Financial Crisis

The 2008 financial crisis did not remain confined to the United States; it had profound and far-reaching effects on economies around the world. Here's how the crisis impacted various regions:

- **United Kingdom:** The UK experienced a severe recession due to the GFC. Major banks like Royal Bank of Scotland (RBS) and Lloyds had to be bailed out by the government to prevent their collapse. The property market declined sharply, and unemployment rose significantly. The UK government implemented austerity measures to reduce its budget deficit, which affected public services and welfare programs.

- **Austerity Explained:** Austerity refers to government policies aimed at reducing public spending and budget deficits, often through spending cuts or tax increases. A budget deficit occurs when a government spends more money than it receives in revenue. In the UK, austerity measures led to significant cuts in public services. For example, funding for local councils was reduced, leading to cuts in social care services and public libraries, impacting communities across the country.

- **Europe:** The crisis exposed vulnerabilities in the European banking sector and led to the Eurozone debt crisis. Countries like Greece, Ireland, Portugal, Spain, and Italy faced severe financial instability, with Greece requiring multiple bailout packages from the International Monetary Fund (IMF) and the European Union (EU). Austerity measures and structural reforms were implemented across these nations, leading to widespread social unrest and economic hardship.

Structural Reforms Explained: Structural reforms are policies aimed at improving the long-term efficiency and productivity of an economy. These can include labour market reforms, changes to pension systems, and improvements in regulatory frameworks. In Greece, for example, structural reforms included pension cuts and labour market deregulation. Real-world examples of social unrest include mass protests in Greece against austerity measures and high unemployment rates, and significant public demonstrations in Spain's "Indignados" movement against economic inequality and austerity policies.

- **China:** While China was not directly affected by the collapse of financial institutions, the GFC led to a significant decline in global demand for Chinese exports. To counteract the slowdown, the Chinese government launched a massive stimulus package focused on infrastructure and real estate development. This helped to maintain high growth rates but also contributed to concerns about a property bubble in China. Excessive investment in real estate led to overbuilding, creating numerous vacant properties and raising fears of a potential market correction.

- **Japan:** Japan, already dealing with economic stagnation from its own banking crisis in the 1990s, was hit hard by the GFC. The country experienced a sharp decline in exports, leading to a recession. The Japanese government responded with fiscal stimulus measures and monetary easing.

Fiscal Stimulus and Monetary Easing Explained: A fiscal stimulus involves increased government spending and tax cuts to boost economic activity. Monetary easing, also known as monetary policy easing, involves lowering interest rates and increasing the money supply to encourage borrowing and investment. Despite these measures, the crisis prolonged Japan's economic challenges, making it difficult to achieve sustained growth.

Emerging Markets (EMs): Emerging markets, including countries in Latin America, Asia, and Africa, faced varying degrees of impact from the GFC. Many experienced capital outflows as investors sought safe-haven assets. Commodity-exporting countries like Brazil and Russia saw declines in prices for their exports, leading to economic slowdowns.

Capital Outflows and Safe-Haven Assets Explained: Capital outflows refer to the movement of money out of a country as investors withdraw their investments. Safe-haven assets are investments considered low risk during times of economic uncertainty, such as gold and government bonds. Commodities are raw materials or primary agricultural products that can be bought and sold, like oil, gold, and agricultural goods.

The 2008 financial crisis was a complex and severe economic event triggered by the collapse of the housing bubble and exacerbated by the widespread issuance of subprime mortgages. The crisis led to significant financial turmoil, with major institutions like Lehman Brothers collapsing and global markets experiencing severe distress. The Federal Reserve, along with the U.S. government, implemented a range of measures, including lowering interest rates, quantitative easing, emergency lending facilities, and the nationalization of Fannie Mae and Freddie Mac, to stabilize the economy and prevent a complete financial collapse. The crisis also led to significant regulatory reforms aimed at preventing future financial disasters. Understanding these actions and their implications is crucial to comprehending how the global financial system operates and responds to crises. The GFC's global impact underscores the interconnectedness of modern economies and the importance of international cooperation in addressing financial instability.

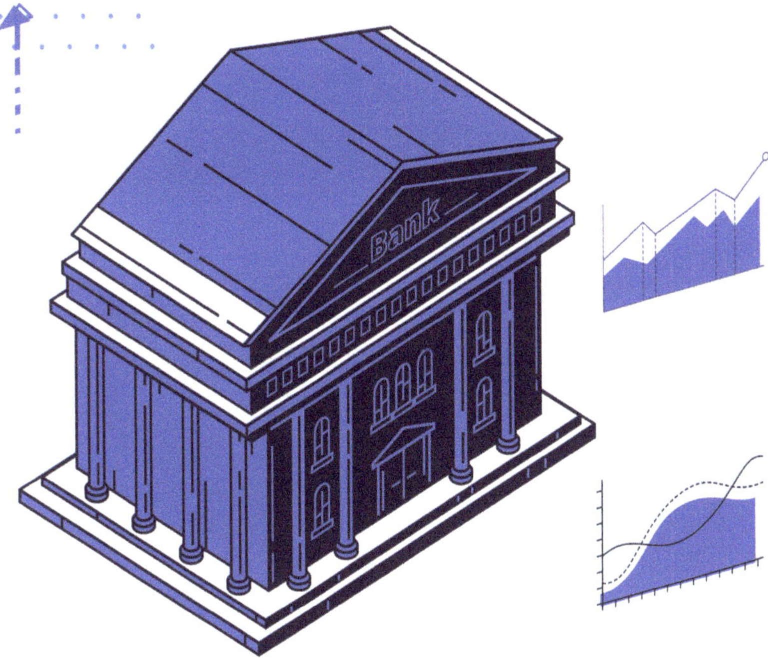

During the 2008 financial crisis, central banks around the world coordinated closely to stabilize the global financial system. Key actions included:

Coordinated Rate Cuts: Major central banks, including the Federal Reserve, the ECB, the Bank of England, and others, simultaneously cut interest rates to provide liquidity and support economic activity.

Currency Swap Lines: Central banks established currency swap lines to ensure the availability of U.S. dollars and other major currencies in global markets. This helped stabilize exchange rates and provided liquidity to banks outside the U.S.

The long-term impacts of the coordinated actions taken during the 2008 financial crisis, including the establishment of currency swap lines, have been significant. These swap lines, originally set up as emergency measures, have now become a more permanent feature of the global financial system. Before swap lines, central banks had limited ways to access foreign currencies quickly, which often led to severe liquidity shortages and increased financial instability during crises. Most central banks heavily relied on the U.S. dollar, with some countries conducting almost all of their international trade exclusively in dollars.

For example, many countries in Latin America and Asia primarily used the U.S. dollar for their trade and financial transactions, making them highly dependent on U.S. monetary policy. Now, with swap lines in place, central banks can more easily exchange a variety of currencies, providing a reliable safety net and enhancing global financial stability.

These relatively newly established swap lines have had several lasting effects:

Enhanced Stability and Confidence: The establishment of swap lines has enhanced the stability of the global financial system by providing a safety net. Central banks now have a mechanism to quickly access foreign currencies in times of crisis, which helps prevent liquidity shortages and reduces the risk of financial contagion.

Strengthened International Cooperation: The crisis fostered a spirit of cooperation among central banks, which has persisted. This cooperation has led to better coordination of monetary policies and a greater ability to respond collectively to global financial challenges.

Reduced Reliance on the U.S. Dollar: While the U.S. dollar remains the dominant global reserve currency, the existence of swap lines has provided central banks with more flexibility. They can access other major currencies more easily, which may slightly reduce their reliance on the U.S. dollar in times of stress. However, the dollar's role as the primary reserve currency is still firmly entrenched.

Normalization of Swap Lines: What started as emergency measures have become more normalized. Central banks, especially those in major economies, now view swap lines as a standard tool for maintaining financial stability, not just an emergency measure.

Broader Implications for Monetary Policy: The use of swap lines and other crisis measures has expanded the toolkit of central banks. They now have more tools at their disposal to manage financial stability and ensure liquidity in the global financial system.

While swap lines have provided central banks with additional options and enhanced global financial stability, they have not significantly reduced the central role of the U.S. dollar in the international financial system. The dollar remains the world's primary reserve currency, meaning it is the most widely held currency by governments and institutions as part of their foreign exchange reserves.

Primary Reserve Currency Explained

A primary reserve currency is one that is held in significant quantities by governments and institutions as part of their foreign exchange reserves. These reserves are used to back a country's own currency, pay off international debt, and influence the exchange rate. The U.S. dollar holds this position due to several factors, including the size and strength of the U.S. economy, the stability of the U.S. political system, trust in U.S. financial markets, and the military strength of the United States.

Benefits for the United States

Having the U.S. dollar as the primary reserve currency provides several advantages for the United States:

1. **Lower Borrowing Costs:** The U.S. can borrow money at lower interest rates because there is high demand for U.S. debt. Countries and institutions around the world buy U.S. Treasury bonds to hold as reserves.

2. **Economic Stability:** The high demand for dollars helps to keep the currency stable. This stability attracts investment from around the world.
3. **Trade Benefits:** Many international transactions are conducted in dollars, which simplifies trade for U.S. businesses.
4. **Financial Influence:** The U.S. has significant influence over global financial markets and can implement sanctions more effectively by restricting access to the dollar.

Why the Dollar Holds This Position

The dollar remains dominant due to several key reasons:

1. **Economic Size:** The U.S. economy is the largest in the world, which makes the dollar a natural choice for international trade and finance.
2. **Stability and Trust:** The U.S. has a long history of political stability and a strong legal system, which builds trust in the dollar.
3. **Liquidity:** The U.S. financial markets are deep and liquid, meaning they can handle large transactions without much impact on the currency's value.
4. **Military Strength:** The U.S. military presence around the world helps ensure geopolitical stability, which in turn supports economic stability. The military helps protect international trade routes, ensuring the free flow of goods and services. Additionally, the ability to enforce economic sanctions effectively supports the dollar's dominance.

Challenges to the Dollar's Dominance

While the U.S. dollar remains dominant, there are potential challengers:

1. **Euro:** The euro is the second most held reserve currency. The European Union's large economy and strong financial markets make it a contender.
2. **Chinese Yuan**: China is actively promoting the yuan for international use. However, concerns about the Chinese government's control over the currency and financial markets limit its appeal.
3. **Cryptocurrencies:** Digital currencies like Bitcoin have gained attention, but they are not yet stable or widely accepted enough to challenge traditional reserve currencies.

In summary, while swap lines have given central banks more tools to manage financial stability, they have not reduced the central role of the U.S. dollar in the global economy. The dollar remains the primary reserve currency, providing significant benefits to the United States, including lower borrowing costs and greater economic stability. This dominance is supported by the size and strength of the U.S. economy, its political stability, the trust in its financial markets, and its military strength. Despite potential challenges from other currencies, the dollar's position remains strong.

Understanding the Great Depression

The Great Depression was a severe worldwide economic depression that took place during the 1930s, beginning in the United States. It was the longest, deepest, and most widespread depression of the 20th century. The depression originated in the United States after a major fall in stock prices that began around September 4, 1929, and became worldwide news with the stock market crash of October 29, 1929, known as Black Tuesday.

The Stock Market Crash of 1929

Stock Market Boom: In the years leading up to the Great Depression, the U.S. stock market experienced a massive boom. The 1920s, known as the "Roaring Twenties," were a time of great economic prosperity, and stock prices soared. Many people borrowed money to buy stocks, a practice known as buying on margin, expecting stock prices to continue rising.

Black Tuesday: On October 29, 1929, stock prices collapsed. Billions of dollars were lost, wiping out thousands of investors. The crash marked the beginning of a decade-long economic downturn. Before the crash, the U.S. stock market was worth approximately $87 billion (equivalent to about $1.35 trillion today); by 1932, it had lost nearly 90% of its value.

Example: A factory worker in New York might have invested his life savings of $2,000 (around $31,000 today) in the stock market, seeing it as a sure way to wealth. When the market crashed, his savings were wiped out overnight, leaving him and his family in financial ruin.

Bank Failures and the Banking Crisis

Bank Runs: After the stock market crash, many banks experienced runs, where large numbers of people withdrew their deposits because they feared the bank would become insolvent. Insolvent means that the bank does not have enough money to cover all the deposits people have made. This caused many banks to collapse, further exacerbating the economic crisis.

Banking Crisis: Between 1930 and 1933, nearly half of the banks in the United States failed. The failure of so many banks led to a significant contraction in the money supply, worsening the economic situation.

Contraction in the Money Supply Explained: The money supply is the total amount of money available in an economy at a particular time, including cash, coins, and balances held in checking and savings accounts. A contraction in the money supply means that there is less money circulating in the economy. This happens when banks fail because they can no longer lend money or return deposits to customers.

When a bank fails, the money deposited in it can essentially disappear if the bank doesn't have sufficient reserves to pay back its depositors. If many banks fail simultaneously, a significant amount of money is removed from the economy. Additionally, as confidence in the banking system erodes, people hoard cash rather than depositing it, further reducing the money in circulation.

This reduction in the money supply leads to several negative effects:

- **Deflation:** With less money available, prices of goods and services tend to fall. While this might sound beneficial, deflation can actually harm the economy because consumers and businesses delay spending and investment, expecting prices to fall further.

- **Reduced Spending:** People and businesses have less money to spend, leading to decreased demand for goods and services. This reduction in spending causes businesses to cut back on production and lay off workers, increasing unemployment.

- **Credit Crunch:** With fewer banks operating and those that remain being more cautious, it becomes much harder for businesses and individuals to obtain loans. This credit crunch further hampers economic activity as businesses cannot invest in new projects or expand, and consumers cannot finance large purchases like homes or cars.

Example: A small construction company in Illinois might have struggled to secure a loan to complete a housing project. Without the necessary funds, the company had to halt construction, lay off workers, and delay payments to suppliers, creating a ripple effect of economic distress.

The Federal Reserve's Response

Initial Inaction: The Federal Reserve, the central banking system of the United States, was initially passive in responding to the crisis. It did not increase the money supply or provide sufficient support to failing banks.

Monetary Policy Mistakes: The Fed's failure to act aggressively led to a deflationary spiral, where falling prices led to reduced consumer spending and investment, which in turn led to further declines in prices and economic activity.

Real-World Example: A local grocery store in Boston might have seen its sales plummet as people spent less money. Falling prices for food meant the store earned less income, leading to layoffs and reduced orders from suppliers.

Government Response and New Deal Programs

Herbert Hoover's Policies: President Herbert Hoover initially responded with limited government intervention, believing that the economy would recover on its own. However, the economic situation continued to deteriorate.

Franklin D. Roosevelt and the New Deal: In 1933, Franklin D. Roosevelt became president and implemented the New Deal, a series of programs and reforms designed to revive the economy and provide relief to the unemployed.

New Deal Programs

- **Works Progress Administration (WPA):** Created jobs for millions of unemployed Americans by funding public works projects such as roads, schools, and bridges.

- **Civilian Conservation Corps (CCC):** The CCC was a public work relief program that operated from 1933 to 1942 in the United States for unemployed, unmarried men. The program provided jobs related to the conservation and development of natural resources in rural lands owned by federal, state, and local governments. Projects included planting trees, building flood barriers, fighting forest fires, and maintaining forest roads and trails.

- **Social Security Act:** Established a system of old-age benefits and unemployment insurance. Old-age benefits are regular payments made to retired workers aged 65 or older, providing them with a source of income in their retirement years. Unemployment insurance provides temporary financial assistance to workers who have lost their jobs through no fault of their own, helping them to meet their basic needs while they search for new employment.

Example: A young man in rural Alabama might have found work through the CCC, planting trees and building infrastructure, providing him with income (about $30 a month, equivalent to roughly $600 today) and a sense of purpose.

Global Impact of the Great Depression

The Great Depression did not remain confined to the United States; it had profound and far-reaching effects on economies around the world. Here's how the crisis impacted various regions:

United Kingdom: The UK experienced a severe economic downturn during the Great Depression. Unemployment rose sharply, particularly in industrial areas. The UK economy was closely linked to the U.S. economy through trade and investment. The depression led to a significant drop in British exports, as demand in the United States and other countries declined. Additionally, American loans that had been crucial to British economic stability were recalled, putting further strain on the UK economy.

To combat the crisis, the UK government implemented austerity measures aimed at reducing the budget deficit. These measures included cuts to public spending and increases in taxes. The budget deficit occurs when a government spends more money than it receives, leading to borrowing to cover the shortfall. The austerity measures led to significant cuts in public services and welfare programs, worsening the economic hardship for many British citizens.

Implications of Austerity Measures:

- Reduced Public Services: Funding for healthcare, education, and social services was significantly cut. For example, public health services saw reduced funding, leading to longer waiting times for medical care and fewer resources for hospitals.

- Social Unrest: The economic hardship and reductions in public services led to widespread social unrest. Protests and strikes became common as people demanded better working conditions and government support.

Europe: The economic depression spread to Europe, where many countries faced severe financial instability. Germany, already burdened with reparations from World War I, was hit particularly hard.

Reparations Explained: Reparations are payments made by a defeated country to the victors to compensate for damages caused during a war. After World War I, Germany was required to pay significant reparations to the Allied countries, primarily France and Belgium. These reparations were set at 132 billion gold marks (approximately $33 billion at the time, which is around $528 billion today). The burden of these payments severely strained the German economy, contributing to hyperinflation and economic instability.

In Germany, the economic crisis contributed to the rise of extremist political movements. The Nazi Party, led by Adolf Hitler, capitalized on the economic despair and promised economic recovery and national renewal. Structural reforms were implemented, including labour market reforms and changes to the pension system, aimed at improving economic efficiency and productivity. The economic instability and political turmoil created fertile ground for radical ideologies, leading to the eventual outbreak of World War II.

Economic instability often leads to radicalism as people look for someone to blame for their hardships. This can result in increased violence, social unrest, and, in extreme cases, wars and genocides. The desperation and anger during the Great Depression provided a platform for radical leaders who promised quick solutions and scapegoated minorities or foreign nations.

The Great Depression was a complex and severe economic event triggered by the stock market crash of 1929 and exacerbated by a series of banking failures and inadequate policy responses. The depression led to significant financial turmoil, with major institutions collapsing and global markets experiencing severe distress. The U.S. government, under President Franklin D. Roosevelt, implemented a range of measures, including the New Deal programs, to stabilize the economy and provide relief to the unemployed. The crisis also led to significant regulatory reforms aimed at preventing future financial disasters. Understanding these actions and their implications is crucial to comprehending how the global financial system operates and responds to crises. The Great Depression's global impact underscores the interconnectedness of modern economies and the importance of international cooperation in addressing financial instability.

Understanding the Eurozone Debt Crisis

The Eurozone debt crisis was a major economic issue that started in Europe around 2009, right after a global financial meltdown. Several countries in Europe, like Greece, Portugal, Ireland, Spain, and Italy, had borrowed a lot of money. They struggled to pay back what they owed because their economies weren't strong enough.

Causes of the Eurozone Debt Crisis

These countries all use the same currency, called the euro, but each had different financial situations. Some had too much debt and weak economies, so they couldn't grow enough to pay off their loans.

Greece had accumulated significant debt due to years of overspending and tax evasion. The government was responsible for much of this overspending, which included extensive public sector wages, generous pension plans, and large infrastructure projects such as the 2004 Athens Olympics. These expenditures were not matched by tax revenues, partly because of widespread tax evasion among the wealthy and even among smaller business owners. The Greek government struggled to enforce tax laws effectively, leading to a significant shortfall in revenue. When the global financial crisis hit, Greece's economy contracted sharply, making it impossible for the government to pay its creditors, which included international banks, the European Central Bank (ECB), and the International Monetary Fund (IMF).

The inability to pay creditors led to a severe crisis of confidence in Greece's financial stability. The country was forced to seek international bailouts, which came with stringent austerity measures. These measures included severe cuts to public spending, tax increases, and structural reforms aimed at improving fiscal responsibility and economic competitiveness. Fiscal responsibility refers to the government's ability to manage its budget by ensuring that spending does not exceed revenue. It involves making sustainable economic decisions, reducing debt levels, and ensuring long-term economic stability. The social implications were severe, with widespread unemployment, poverty, and social unrest. Public services were slashed, and many Greeks faced significant hardship.

Ireland: Ireland's crisis was primarily rooted in a massive housing bubble that burst. During the early 2000s, Ireland experienced a property boom, with banks lending excessively to property developers and homebuyers. When the bubble burst, property prices plummeted, leading to a banking crisis. Irish banks were left with huge amounts of bad debt, and the government had to step in to bail out the banks, significantly increasing the national debt. The Irish government implemented austerity measures, including cuts to public sector wages, increases in taxes, and reductions in public spending, to stabilize the economy. The European Union and the International Monetary Fund provided bailout funds to help Ireland manage its debt and recapitalize its banks.

IMF Explained: The International Monetary Fund (IMF) is an international financial institution that provides loans and financial assistance to countries facing economic difficulties. It aims to stabilize international monetary systems and foster global financial cooperation. The IMF imposes conditions on the borrowing countries, which typically include implementing economic reforms to ensure financial stability and repayment of the loans.

Portugal: Portugal faced a combination of low economic growth, high government debt, and inefficient public sectors. Years of sluggish economic performance and poor fiscal management left the country vulnerable. The global financial crisis exacerbated these issues, leading to a severe recession. The Portuguese government implemented austerity measures, including public sector wage cuts, pension reforms, and tax increases, to reduce the budget deficit. Portugal received financial assistance from the European Union and the International Monetary Fund, which helped stabilize the economy and restore investor confidence.

Spain: Spain's crisis was similar to Ireland's, with a massive housing bubble playing a central role. During the early 2000s, Spain experienced a construction boom, fuelled by easy credit and speculative investments in real estate. Investors, including banks, developers, and individuals, were heavily involved in speculative investing, buying properties with the hope that prices would continue to rise. When the bubble burst, property prices collapsed, leading to a banking crisis. Spanish banks were left with significant bad debts, and the government had to step in to support the financial sector. The Spanish government implemented austerity measures, including cuts to public spending, tax increases, and labour market reforms, to stabilize the economy. Labour market reforms aimed at making it easier for businesses to hire and fire employees, reducing labour costs, and increasing flexibility in employment contracts. The European Union provided financial assistance to recapitalize Spanish banks and restore confidence in the financial system.

Italy: Italy's crisis was driven by high public debt and low economic growth. The country had accumulated significant debt over the years, partly due to extensive public spending and an inefficient tax system. When the global financial crisis hit, Italy's economy contracted, making it difficult for the government to manage its debt. The Italian government implemented austerity measures, including pension reforms, public sector wage cuts, and tax increases, to reduce the budget deficit. Italy also undertook structural reforms aimed at improving economic competitiveness and productivity. These structural reforms included measures to simplify regulations, promote business investment, and increase labour market flexibility. The European Central Bank's intervention, including lowering interest rates and purchasing government bonds, helped stabilize the situation and restore investor confidence.

Government Responses and International Assistance

The European Central Bank (ECB) played a crucial role in stabilizing the situation by:

1. **Lowering Central Bank Rates:**
   - The ECB reduced the cost of short-term borrowing for banks. Lowering the central bank rates made it cheaper for banks to borrow money, which was intended to encourage them to lend more to businesses and consumers.
2. **Providing Liquidity:**
   - The ECB offered loans to banks through long-term refinancing operations (LTROs). LTROs provided banks with cheap, long-term loans, ensuring they had enough liquidity to continue their operations and lend to the economy.

LTROs Explained: Long-Term Refinancing Operations are mechanisms by which the ECB provides financing to eurozone banks. Banks can borrow funds at a low interest rate, with the loan typically lasting several years. This helps banks manage their liquidity needs and supports lending to businesses and households.

Example: A Spanish bank could participate in an LTRO to secure a multi-year loan at a low interest rate, which it could then use to support mortgage lending and business loans.

3. **Purchasing Bonds:**
   - The ECB launched the Securities Markets Programme (SMP) to purchase sovereign debt, lowering borrowing costs for distressed countries.

SMP Explained: Under the SMP, the ECB bought government bonds from troubled eurozone countries. By purchasing these bonds, the ECB aimed to reduce the yields (interest rates) on them, making it cheaper for these countries to borrow money.

How Bonds Work: Bonds are essentially loans made by investors to governments or corporations. When a government issues a bond, it promises to pay back the loan amount (principal) on a specific date (maturity) and make periodic interest payments (coupons) along the way. Governments use bonds to finance their operations, such as funding public projects or managing debt. By purchasing government bonds, the ECB helped reduce borrowing costs for countries like Greece, providing them with more affordable access to funds needed to manage their debt and finance public services.

The Role of the IMF

The International Monetary Fund (IMF) played a significant role during the Eurozone debt crisis by providing financial assistance and imposing economic reforms. The IMF's involvement typically involves the following:

1. **Financial Assistance:** The IMF provides loans to countries facing economic crises, helping them stabilize their economies and restore confidence in their financial systems.
2. **Conditions and Reforms:** In exchange for financial assistance, the IMF imposes conditions on the borrowing countries. These conditions often include implementing economic reforms such as austerity measures, fiscal consolidation, and structural changes to improve economic efficiency and competitiveness.

Fiscal Consolidation Explained: Fiscal consolidation refers to policies aimed at reducing government deficits and debt accumulation. This typically involves increasing taxes, reducing public spending, or a combination of both to achieve a more sustainable fiscal position.

3. **Short-Term Effects:** The immediate impact of IMF involvement can include reduced government spending, increased taxes, and other austerity measures. These can lead to economic contraction, higher unemployment, and social unrest.

4. **Long-Term Effects:** Over time, the economic reforms mandated by the IMF can lead to improved fiscal stability, increased investor confidence, and more sustainable economic growth. However, the short-term pain can be severe, and the social and political implications can be significant.
5. **IMF's Mission:** The IMF aims to promote international monetary cooperation, secure financial stability, facilitate international trade, promote high employment and sustainable economic growth, and reduce poverty around the world.

The Eurozone debt crisis was a significant economic challenge that emerged in the wake of the global financial crisis. European countries with high levels of debt and weak economies, such as Greece, Portugal, Ireland, Spain, and Italy, faced severe financial difficulties. The crisis led to austerity measures, social unrest, and economic hardship across the affected nations. The European Central Bank played a crucial role in stabilizing the situation by lowering central bank rates, providing liquidity through LTROs, and purchasing government bonds. The International Monetary Fund also played a critical role by providing financial assistance and imposing economic reforms. Understanding the Eurozone debt crisis highlights the complexities of interconnected economies and the importance of coordinated policy responses in addressing financial instability.

Economic Indicators used by Central Banks

Economic Indicators Used by Central Banks

Economic Indicators Used by the Federal Reserve

The Federal Reserve uses a wide range of economic indicators to guide its decisions and ensure the U.S. economy remains healthy. A healthy economy is one where there is steady growth, low unemployment, stable prices, and confidence among consumers and businesses. These indicators help the Federal Reserve determine when to adjust interest rates, use tools like quantitative easing or tightening, and take other actions such as setting reserve requirements and implementing open market operations to manage the economy. By monitoring these indicators, the Federal Reserve can respond to economic trends and keep things stable, which means maintaining balance in the economy to avoid issues like high inflation or recession.

Inflation Rate

- **Consumer Price Index (CPI):** This measures how much the prices of everyday items like food, clothing, and transportation have changed over time. A "basket of goods and services" includes a variety of items that households commonly buy, such as groceries, housing, clothes, transportation, healthcare, and education. The CPI is calculated by taking price changes for each item in the basket and averaging them, with the items weighted according to their importance. It is calculated and reported by the Bureau of Labour Statistics (BLS).
- **Producer Price Index (PPI):** This tracks changes in the prices that businesses receive for their products, which can be a sign of future changes in consumer prices. It measures price changes from the perspective of the seller. The PPI is calculated by surveying producers and tracking the prices they receive for their output. It is also calculated by the BLS.
- **Personal Consumption Expenditures (PCE) Price Index:** This measures the prices people pay for goods and services, including healthcare and education. The PCE Price Index is calculated by taking the total amount spent on a specific basket of goods and services and dividing it by the total quantity of those goods and services. It is calculated and reported by the Bureau of Economic Analysis (BEA).

Unemployment Rate

- **Nonfarm Payrolls:** This shows how many jobs were added or lost, not counting farm jobs. Farm jobs are excluded because they tend to be seasonal and can fluctuate widely depending on the time of year, which can distort the overall employment picture. Nonfarm payrolls are calculated by the Bureau of Labour Statistics (BLS) through monthly surveys of businesses and government agencies.

- **Jobless Claims:** This tells us how many people are applying for unemployment benefits. It is calculated by tallying the number of new claims filed each week by individuals seeking unemployment insurance. This data is reported by the U.S. Department of Labour.
- **Labour Force Participation Rate:** This is the percentage of people who are either working or actively looking for work. It is calculated by dividing the labour force (the sum of employed and unemployed people actively seeking work) by the working-age population. This information is provided by the BLS.

Gross Domestic Product (GDP)

- **Real GDP:** This is the total value of everything produced in the country, adjusted for price changes (inflation). For example, it includes cars made in factories, software developed by tech companies, and services provided by healthcare workers. Real GDP is calculated by taking the nominal GDP and adjusting it for inflation using a price index. It is calculated and reported by the Bureau of Economic Analysis (BEA).
- **Nominal GDP:** This measures the total value of all goods and services produced at current prices, without adjusting for inflation. It is calculated by summing up the market values of all final goods and services produced within a country in a given period. It is also reported by the BEA.

Interest Rates

- **Federal Funds Rate:** This is the interest rate at which banks lend money to each other overnight. The Federal Reserve sets a target for this rate, which influences other interest rates in the economy. The Federal Open Market Committee (FOMC) of the Federal Reserve determines this rate.
- **Long-term Interest Rates:** These are interest rates on loans and bonds that last many years, affecting mortgages, corporate bonds, and government debt. They are determined by the supply and demand for credit in the financial markets and are tracked by financial institutions and reported by entities such as the Federal Reserve.
- **Yield Curve:** A graph that shows the difference between short-term and long-term interest rates. The yield curve is calculated by plotting interest rates of bonds with different maturities, such as 3-month, 2-year, 10-year, and 30-year bonds. It is typically published by financial institutions and government agencies like the U.S. Department of the Treasury.

Consumer Confidence Index (CCI)

- This measures how optimistic or pessimistic consumers are about the economy. It is calculated based on surveys that ask people about their views on current and future economic conditions. The Conference Board, a non-profit research organization, is one of the primary entities that calculate and publish the CCI.

Retail Sales

- This shows the total sales made by retail stores, indicating how much consumers are spending. It is calculated by the Census Bureau through monthly surveys of retailers.

Industrial Production

- This measures the output of factories, mines, and utilities. It is calculated by the Federal Reserve using data from various sources, including industry reports and surveys.

Housing Market Indicators

- **Housing Starts:** The number of new homes being built. It is calculated by the Census Bureau through monthly surveys of homebuilders.
- **Building Permits:** The number of permits issued for new construction. It is a leading indicator of future construction activity and is also calculated by the Census Bureau.
- **Home Sales:** The number of new and existing homes sold. It is reported by the National Association of Realtors and other housing authorities.

Balance of Trade

- The balance of trade is the difference between the value of a country's exports (goods sold to other countries) and imports (goods bought from other countries). It is calculated by subtracting the value of imports from the value of exports. If a country exports more than it imports, it has a trade surplus. Conversely, if it imports more than it exports, it has a trade deficit. This data is reported by the Bureau of Economic Analysis (BEA). The balance of trade is an important indicator of a country's economic health and its position in the global market. A trade surplus can indicate strong production and competitiveness, while a trade deficit might suggest reliance on foreign goods and accumulation of debt. However, a trade surplus is not always a sign of a healthy economy. For example, in Japan during the 1990s, the country had a significant trade surplus but was experiencing economic stagnation, known as the "Lost Decade." This was due to weak domestic demand and overreliance on exports, which did not translate into robust economic growth within the country.

Money Supply

- Money supply is measured in M1, M2, and M3:
  - **M1:** The most liquid forms of money, including cash and checking deposits.
  - **M2:** Includes all of M1 plus savings accounts, small time deposits, and retail money market funds.

- **M3:** Includes all of M2 plus large time deposits, institutional money market funds, and other larger liquid assets.

- These measures show how much money is available in the economy, which affects inflation and economic activity. They are denoted this way to differentiate between the levels of liquidity and availability of funds in the economy. The Federal Reserve publishes this data.

Business Inventories

- The amount of goods that businesses have in stock. It indicates future production activity, as low inventories may lead to increased production. It is calculated by the Census Bureau through monthly surveys of manufacturers, wholesalers, and retailers.

Purchasing Managers' Index (PMI)

- An indicator of the economic health of the manufacturing sector. It is based on surveys of private-sector companies, covering new orders, inventory levels, production, supplier deliveries, and employment. The PMI is calculated by compiling responses from purchasing managers and expressing the results as a diffusion index. This index is produced by the Institute for Supply Management (ISM) in the United States.

Exchange Rates

- The value of a country's currency compared to another currency. Exchange rates affect trade balances and economic stability. They are determined by the foreign exchange market, where currencies are traded.

Commodity Prices

- Prices of important goods like oil, gold, and agricultural products. These prices affect inflation and the cost of goods. They are tracked by commodity exchanges and reported by various financial news services.

Budget Deficit/Surplus

- The difference between what the government spends and what it earns in revenue (money collected from taxes, fees, and other sources). A deficit occurs when spending exceeds revenue, and a surplus occurs when revenue exceeds spending. Governments fund their spending through taxes, borrowing, and sometimes printing money. For example, if the government spends $1 trillion but only collects

$900 billion in taxes, it has a deficit of $100 billion. This data is reported by the U.S. Department of the Treasury.

Current Account Balance

- The difference between a nation's savings and its investment. It includes trade balance, net income from abroad, and net current transfers. Nations save by holding reserves in foreign currencies, gold, or other financial assets. A surplus indicates a nation is a net lender to the rest of the world, while a deficit indicates it is a net borrower. This information is calculated and reported by the Bureau of Economic Analysis (BEA).

Debt-to-GDP Ratio

- This measures a country's debt compared to its economic output (GDP). It indicates the country's ability to pay back its debt. Economic output refers to the total value of all goods and services produced in the country. A high ratio means the country has a lot of debt compared to its economic output, which can be risky. For example, if a country has $20 trillion in debt and a GDP of $25 trillion, its debt-to-GDP ratio is 80%. Increasing ratios worldwide raise concerns about sustainability, as high debt levels can limit a country's ability to invest in growth and may lead to higher borrowing costs. This data is reported by the International Monetary Fund (IMF) and other financial organizations.

Savings Rate

- The portion of income that people save instead of spending. It indicates future spending capacity and financial health of households. It is calculated by the Bureau of Economic Analysis (BEA) using data on personal income and expenditures.

Corporate Profits

- The earnings of companies. High profits suggest business health and can lead to increased investment and hiring. It is reported by companies in their financial statements and aggregated by the BEA.

Productivity

- The output per worker or per hour worked. Higher productivity means more efficient production and economic growth. It is calculated by the Bureau of Labour Statistics (BLS) using data on output and hours worked.

Capacity Utilization

- How much of a country's production capacity is being used. It indicates the level of demand and potential inflationary pressures. It is calculated by the Federal Reserve using data on industrial production and capacity.

Inflation Expectations

- Predictions of future inflation rates. They influence consumer behaviour and wage negotiations. They are measured through surveys and market-based indicators like inflation-protected securities.

Phillips Curve

- The Phillips Curve illustrates the inverse relationship between unemployment and inflation. Historically, it suggested that as unemployment decreases, inflation increases, and vice versa. This relationship was based on the observation that low unemployment often led to higher wages, which in turn increased inflation. However, recent economic experiences, such as during the 2000s and 2010s, have led to a reevaluation of its usefulness as a predictive tool. For instance, the U.S. experienced low unemployment and low inflation simultaneously, challenging the traditional Phillips Curve model. Economists now consider other factors like globalization, technological advancements, and changes in labour market dynamics, which can influence both inflation and unemployment independently. The Federal Reserve now uses a broader set of indicators to predict inflation and guide policy decisions.

Real-World Example: Federal Reserve's Interest Rate Decision in 2024

In 2024, the Federal Reserve decided to keep interest rates unchanged. This decision was based on a comprehensive analysis of several key economic indicators:

- **Inflation Rate:** The Consumer Price Index (CPI) and Personal Consumption Expenditures (PCE) Price Index showed moderate inflation, indicating that prices for goods and services were rising at a controlled pace. This suggested that there was no immediate need to raise interest rates to curb inflation.

- **Unemployment Rate:** The unemployment rate remained low, with strong job growth across various sectors. Nonfarm payrolls data showed steady job creation, indicating a healthy labour market.

- **GDP Growth Rate:** The GDP growth rate was stable, reflecting balanced economic expansion. The Federal Reserve considered this a sign that the economy was growing at a sustainable rate without overheating.

- **Consumer Confidence Index (CCI):** Consumer confidence remained high, suggesting that people felt optimistic about the economy and their personal financial situations. High consumer confidence usually translates to increased spending, which supports economic growth.

- **Retail Sales:** Retail sales data indicated robust consumer spending, further supporting the decision to maintain the current interest rates.

- **Industrial Production:** The output from factories, mines, and utilities showed consistent growth, indicating strong industrial activity.

- **Housing Market Indicators:** Housing starts and building permits data revealed a healthy housing market, with stable growth in new home construction.

Decision to Keep Interest Rates Unchanged

The decision to keep interest rates unchanged was influenced by the combination of stable inflation, strong job growth, balanced GDP growth, high consumer confidence, robust retail sales, strong industrial production, and a healthy housing market. The Federal Reserve concluded that the current economic conditions did not warrant an increase in interest rates, as doing so could potentially slow down the ongoing economic growth.

Short-Term Effects of the Fed's Decision

1. **Stock Market Stability:** The decision to keep interest rates steady provided a sense of stability to the stock market. Investors were reassured that borrowing costs would remain low, which supported higher stock prices.

2. **Consumer Spending:** With interest rates unchanged, borrowing costs for consumers remained low. This encouraged continued spending on big-ticket items like homes and cars, as well as everyday goods and services.

3. **Business Investment:** Low borrowing costs also benefited businesses, making it cheaper to finance new projects, expand operations, and invest in research and development. This supported economic growth and job creation.

4. **Housing Market:** Stable interest rates helped maintain affordability in the housing market, encouraging more home purchases and supporting the construction industry.

5. **Foreign Exchange Rates:** The decision to keep interest rates unchanged had an impact on the value of the U.S. dollar. In a global context, stable interest rates made the dollar an attractive currency for investors seeking stability, influencing foreign exchange markets.

In conclusion, the Federal Reserve's decision to keep interest rates unchanged in 2024 was based on a thorough analysis of various economic indicators. This decision had significant short-term effects on the stock market, consumer spending, business investment, the housing market, and foreign exchange rates, highlighting the substantial impact of the Federal Reserve's actions on the economy.

Economic Indicators Used by the Bank of England (BoE)

The Bank of England (BoE) uses a comprehensive set of economic indicators to guide its decisions and ensure the prosperity of the UK economy. These indicators are crucial for understanding the overall economic environment, including inflation, employment, GDP growth, and financial stability. While both the BoE and the Federal Reserve use similar indicators like GDP and inflation measures, there are differences in their focus areas due to the distinct economic structures of the UK and the US.

For instance, the BoE places significant emphasis on indicators like the Retail Price Index (RPI) and Public Sector Net Borrowing (PSNB), reflecting the UK's specific economic characteristics, such as its public debt levels and the structure of its housing market. In contrast, the Federal Reserve closely monitors indicators like the Personal Consumption Expenditures (PCE) Price Index and Nonfarm Payrolls, which are more reflective of the broader consumer-driven nature of the US economy.

Both central banks use these indicators to make informed decisions on interest rates, manage inflation, and maintain economic stability. However, the BoE's approach is tailored to the unique challenges and opportunities within the UK, ensuring that monetary policy is aligned with the specific needs of the British economy. By monitoring these indicators, the BoE can respond effectively to economic trends, adjusting its policy tools to keep the economy stable and avoid issues such as high inflation, unemployment, or economic recession.

Retail Price Index (RPI) Measures the change in the price of a basket of goods and services, including housing costs like mortgage interest payments. Tracking price changes for each item in the basket and averaging them, with the items weighted according to their importance. The RPI often shows higher inflation rates compared to the CPI due to these inclusions. Reported by the Office for National Statistics (ONS).

Consumer Price Index (CPI) Measures the average change over time in the prices paid by consumers for a basket of goods and services. The CPI is used as the primary measure of inflation in the UK. It is calculated by tracking the prices of a set basket of goods and services over time and averaging the price changes. Reported by the Office for National Statistics (ONS).

Claimant Count Rate Measures the number of people claiming unemployment benefits, providing an immediate snapshot of labour market conditions. Calculated by tallying the total number of claimants each month. Reported by the Office for National Statistics (ONS).

ILO Unemployment Rate The International Labour Organization (ILO) Unemployment Rate measures the percentage of the labour force that is unemployed but actively seeking employment. It is based on the ILO's definition and provides a broader measure of unemployment than the Claimant Count Rate. The ILO is a United Nations agency that sets international labour standards and promotes social justice and fair work conditions worldwide. The ILO's definition of unemployment includes individuals who are without work, currently available for work, and actively seeking work. Reported by the Office for National Statistics (ONS).

House Price Index Tracks changes in the price of residential properties, reflecting the health of the housing market and consumer wealth. Calculated by comparing current prices of sold houses to previous periods. Reported by HM Land Registry and the Office for National Statistics (ONS).

Mortgage Approvals Indicates the number of mortgages approved for house purchases, signalling future housing market activity and consumer confidence. Calculated by tracking the volume of mortgage loan approvals each month. Reported by the Bank of England.

Public Sector Net Borrowing (PSNB) Shows the difference between government spending and revenue, highlighting the government's fiscal position and public sector financial health. Calculated by subtracting total government revenues from total government expenditures. Reported by the Office for National Statistics (ONS).

Money Supply Measured in M0 and M4, indicating the total money available in the economy.

- **M0:** Includes physical currency, calculated by summing up all circulating banknotes and coins. The Bank of England tracks the number of notes and coins issued and monitors their circulation through banks and financial institutions.

- **M4:** A broader measure including various deposits, calculated by adding M0 and all private sector retail and wholesale deposits in the banking system. Reported by the Bank of England.

Gross Domestic Product (GDP) Measures the total value of all goods and services produced within the UK. Real GDP adjusts for inflation, providing a more accurate measure of economic growth. Nominal GDP does not adjust for inflation. Reported by the Office for National Statistics (ONS).

Producer Price Index (PPI) Tracks changes in the prices that businesses receive for their products, which can be a sign of future changes in consumer prices. It measures price changes from the perspective of the seller. Reported by the Office for National Statistics (ONS).

Purchasing Managers' Index (PMI) An indicator of the economic health of the manufacturing sector, based on surveys of private-sector companies covering new orders, inventory levels, production, supplier deliveries, and employment. Reported by IHS Markit and the Chartered Institute of Procurement & Supply (CIPS).

Current Account Balance The difference between a nation's savings and its investment. It includes trade balance, net income from abroad, and net current transfers. A surplus indicates the nation is a net lender, while a deficit indicates it is a net borrower. Reported by the Office for National Statistics (ONS).

Debt-to-GDP Ratio Measures the UK's national debt compared to its GDP, indicating the country's ability to pay back its debt. A high ratio can indicate economic risk. Reported by the Office for National Statistics (ONS).

Inflation Expectations Predictions of future inflation rates, which influence consumer behaviour and wage negotiations. Measured through surveys and market-based indicators like inflation-protected securities. Reported by the Bank of England.

Business Inventories The amount of goods that businesses have in stock, indicating future production activity. Low inventories may lead to increased production. Reported by the Office for National Statistics (ONS).

Exchange Rates The value of the British pound compared to other currencies, affecting trade balances and economic stability. Determined by the foreign exchange market.

Commodity Prices Prices of essential goods like oil, gold, and agricultural products, which affect inflation and the cost of goods. Tracked by commodity exchanges and reported by various financial news services.

Budget Deficit/Surplus The difference between what the government spends and what it earns in revenue (taxes, fees, etc.). A deficit occurs when spending exceeds revenue, and a surplus occurs when revenue exceeds spending. Reported by the Office for National Statistics (ONS).

Savings Rate The portion of income that households save rather than spend. Indicates future spending capacity and financial health. Reported by the Office for National Statistics (ONS).

Real-World Example: Bank of England's Interest Rate Decision in 2023

In 2023, the Bank of England decided to raise interest rates based on a comprehensive analysis of several key economic indicators:

Inflation Rate: The Consumer Price Index (CPI) and Retail Price Index (RPI) showed high inflation, indicating rapidly rising prices for goods and services. This necessitated a rate hike to curb inflation.

Unemployment Rate: The ILO Unemployment Rate was low, with strong job growth across various sectors, indicating a robust labour market that could withstand higher interest rates.

GDP Growth Rate: The GDP growth rate was high, reflecting rapid economic expansion and suggesting the economy was overheating and needed cooling measures like higher interest rates.

Consumer Confidence Index (CCI): Consumer confidence remained high, suggesting optimism about the economy and personal financial situations, but also potentially driving higher spending and contributing to inflation.

Retail Sales: Data indicated strong consumer spending, supporting the decision to raise interest rates to temper demand and control inflation.

House Price Index: Showed significant increases in property prices, indicating potential overheating in the housing market.

Decision to Raise Interest Rates

The decision to raise interest rates was influenced by the combination of high inflation, strong job growth, rapid GDP growth, high consumer confidence, robust retail sales, and rising house prices. The Bank of England concluded that the current economic conditions warranted an increase in interest rates to cool down the economy and prevent runaway inflation.

Short-Term Effects of the BoE's Decision

Stock Market Volatility: The decision to raise interest rates initially led to some volatility in the stock market as investors adjusted to higher borrowing costs and the implications for corporate profits.

Consumer Spending: With higher interest rates, borrowing costs for consumers increased. This discouraged spending on big-ticket items like homes and cars, leading to a slowdown in consumer spending.

Business Investment: Higher borrowing costs also impacted businesses, making it more expensive to finance new projects, expand operations, and invest in research and development. This could potentially slow down economic growth and job creation in the short term.

Housing Market: Higher interest rates led to higher mortgage rates, reducing affordability in the housing market and cooling down the rapid increase in house prices.

Foreign Exchange Rates: The decision to raise interest rates strengthened the British pound as higher interest rates attracted foreign investors seeking better returns.

The Bank of England's decision to raise interest rates in 2023 was based on a thorough analysis of various economic indicators. This decision had significant short-term effects on the stock market, consumer spending, business investment, the housing market, and foreign exchange rates, highlighting the substantial impact of the Bank of England's actions on the economy.

Economic Indicators Used by the European Central Bank (ECB)

The European Central Bank (ECB) utilizes a broad range of economic indicators to guide its monetary policy and ensure economic stability across the Eurozone. These indicators are essential for understanding the diverse economic conditions across member states, including inflation, employment, GDP growth, and financial market stability. While the ECB shares some common indicators with the Federal Reserve and the Bank of England, such as GDP and inflation measures, it uniquely focuses on metrics like the Harmonized Index of Consumer Prices (HICP) and the Euro Area Trade Balance, reflecting the interconnected economies of the Eurozone.

The ECB's approach differs from the Federal Reserve's and the Bank of England's due to the multi-country nature of the Eurozone, requiring a harmonized view of economic conditions across different national contexts. The ECB closely monitors these indicators to make informed decisions on interest rates, manage inflation, and support economic growth across the Eurozone. By doing so, the ECB aims to maintain price stability and foster sustainable economic conditions throughout the member states, balancing the needs of both stronger and weaker economies within the Eurozone.

Harmonized Index of Consumer Prices (HICP)

Measures the average change over time in prices for a standard basket of goods and services across the Eurozone. Reported by Eurostat.

Euro Area Unemployment Rate

Measures the percentage of the labour force unemployed and actively seeking work across the Eurozone. Reported by Eurostat.

Gross Domestic Product (GDP)

Measures the total value of goods and services produced within the Eurozone. Reported by Eurostat.

M3 Money Supply

Reflects the total money available in the Eurozone, including cash, deposits, and liquid assets. Reported by the ECB.

Purchasing Managers' Index (PMI)

An indicator of the health of the manufacturing and services sectors in the Eurozone. Reported by IHS Markit.

Current Account Balance

The difference between the Eurozone's savings and investment, including trade balance and net income from abroad. Reported by Eurostat.

Euro Area Trade Balance

Measures the difference between exports and imports of goods and services in the Eurozone. Reported by Eurostat.

ECB's Main Refinancing Operations Rate (MRO)

The interest rate at which the ECB lends to Eurozone banks, influencing overall interest rates within the region. Reported by the ECB.

Euro Area Industrial Production

Tracks the output of factories, mines, and utilities, reflecting industrial health. Reported by Eurostat.

Long-term Interest Rates

Monitors interest rates on government bonds and other long-term debt within the Eurozone. Reported by national central banks and the ECB.

Euro Area Consumer Confidence Index

Measures consumer optimism or pessimism about the economy across the Eurozone. Reported by the European Commission.

Real-World Example: European Central Bank's Interest Rate Decision in 2023

In 2023, the European Central Bank (ECB) decided to raise interest rates across the Eurozone based on several key economic indicators:

Harmonized Index of Consumer Prices (HICP): The HICP showed a significant increase in inflation across the Eurozone, indicating rising prices for goods and services, prompting the need for a rate hike to control inflation.

Euro Area Unemployment Rate: The unemployment rate was low across the Eurozone, signalling a robust labour market that could absorb the impact of higher interest rates.

GDP Growth Rate: The Eurozone GDP was growing rapidly, suggesting the economy was overheating and could benefit from higher interest rates to prevent excessive inflation.

M3 Money Supply: The broad money supply was expanding quickly, which the ECB saw as a potential driver of future inflation, supporting the decision to raise rates.

Euro Area Trade Balance: The trade balance showed a surplus, indicating a strong export sector, which could help cushion the economy against the effects of higher interest rates.

Decision to Raise Interest Rates in 2023

The ECB's decision to raise interest rates was driven by the combination of rising inflation, strong GDP growth, a robust labour market, and expanding money supply. The ECB aimed to cool the economy and bring inflation back toward its target.

Short-Term Effects of the ECB's 2023 Decision

Financial Market Volatility: The rate hike led to some volatility in financial markets as investors adjusted to the higher cost of borrowing and its potential impact on corporate profits.

Consumer Spending: Higher interest rates increased borrowing costs, leading to a moderation in consumer spending, particularly on big-ticket items like homes and cars.

Business Investment: Businesses faced higher financing costs, which could slow down investment in new projects and expansion efforts, potentially dampening economic growth.

Euro Strengthening: The decision to raise rates contributed to a stronger euro as investors sought higher returns, impacting export competitiveness.

Eurozone Housing Market: Higher mortgage rates led to reduced affordability and a cooling of the housing market in several Eurozone countries.

The ECB's decision to raise interest rates in 2023 was based on a comprehensive analysis of various economic indicators. This decision had significant short-term effects on financial markets, consumer spending, business investment, and the Eurozone economy as a whole, underscoring the impact of the ECB's monetary policy decisions.

Conclusion

Central banks play a vital role in shaping the global economy, They use various complex tools like adjusting interest rates and buying or selling government bonds and other financial instruments to manage how much money is in the system, control inflation, and promote job creation. These actions help ensure that the economy grows at a stable pace, prices remain predictable, and more people can find and keep jobs.

Understanding how central banks work is important for everyone, not just those in finance. When central banks lower interest rates, it becomes cheaper for businesses and individuals to borrow money, which can lead to more spending and investment. On the other hand, when they raise rates, borrowing costs increase, which can help cool down an overheated economy and keep inflation in check.

During times of economic trouble, like the 2008 financial crisis or the COVID-19 pandemic, central banks step in with special measures such as quantitative easing to inject more money into the economy and support financial stability. These actions are crucial in preventing deeper recessions and helping economies recover more quickly.

By learning about these processes, we can better understand the economic news we hear every day and how it impacts our personal finances. Knowing that central banks are working to balance the economy can give us confidence in the stability of our financial system. So, the next time you hear about changes in interest rates or new policies from a central bank, you'll have a better idea of what's happening and why it matters to all of us.

Appendix

Glossary of Key Terms and Concepts

Quantitative Easing (QE):

A monetary policy tool where central banks purchase longer-term securities from the open market to increase the money supply and encourage lending and investment. This lowers long-term interest rates and aims to stimulate economic activity.

Quantitative Tightening (QT):

The opposite of QE, where central banks reduce their holdings of longer-term securities by selling them or letting them mature, decreasing the money supply and raising long-term interest rates to combat inflation.

Reserve Requirements:

Regulations set by central banks that determine the minimum amount of reserves a bank must hold against its deposit liabilities. This influences the amount of money banks can lend out and thus the overall money supply in the economy.

Fed Funds Rate:

The interest rate at which depository institutions lend reserve balances to other depository institutions overnight on an uncollateralized basis. It serves as a benchmark for other interest rates and is a primary tool of U.S. monetary policy.

Overnight Indexed Swap (OIS) Rate:

A rate reflecting the expected average overnight interest rates over the term of the swap. It is used to hedge against interest rate risk.

Eurodollar Market:

A market for U.S. dollars deposited in banks outside the United States. Rates in this market are influenced by the Fed Funds Rate and directly impact global borrowing costs.

LIBOR (London Interbank Offered Rate):

A benchmark rate that was used to set interest rates on various financial instruments, phased out due to manipulation issues and replaced by SOFR.

SOFR (Secured Overnight Financing Rate):

A benchmark interest rate for dollar-denominated derivatives and loans, replacing LIBOR. It is based on the cost of borrowing cash overnight collateralized by Treasury securities.

Prime Rate:

The interest rate that commercial banks charge their most creditworthy customers. It typically follows the Fed Funds Rate closely.

Swap Rate:

The fixed interest rate exchanged for a floating rate (like LIBOR or SOFR) over a specific period in an interest rate swap agreement. It reflects market expectations about future interest rates.

Forward/Futures Rate:

The agreed-upon rate for financial transactions to be conducted at a future date. These rates are derived from expectations about future interest rates, inflation, and economic conditions.

EURIBOR (Euro Interbank Offered Rate):

A benchmark rate that reflects the average interest rate at which eurozone banks are willing to lend unsecured funds to other banks in the euro wholesale money market.

SONIA (Sterling Overnight Index Average):

A benchmark rate for overnight unsecured transactions in the sterling market. It is based on actual transactions and reflects the average interest rate banks pay to borrow sterling overnight.

TONAR (Tokyo Overnight Average Rate):

A Japanese benchmark for overnight unsecured loans. It is based on the weighted average of interest rates of unsecured overnight call transactions.

EONIA (Euro Overnight Index Average):

Previously used for overnight lending in the euro area, EONIA has been largely replaced by €STR (Euro Short-Term Rate), which is based on borrowing costs from eurozone banks.

Derivative:

A financial contract whose value is derived from the performance of underlying assets, indexes, or interest rates. Common derivatives include futures, options, and swaps. Derivatives are used for hedging risk or for speculative purposes.

Repo (Repurchase Agreement):

A form of short-term borrowing where a dealer sells securities (which can include government bonds or other types of securities) to investors, usually on an overnight basis, and buys them back the following day at a slightly higher price. This process effectively provides the seller with short-term capital while offering the buyer a secure, short-term investment. Repos are a common tool for managing short-term liquidity needs in the financial system.

Forward Contract:

A customized contract between two parties to buy or sell an asset at a specified price on a future date. Forwards are not traded on exchanges and are used to hedge risk or speculate.

Futures Contract:

A standardized legal agreement to buy or sell something at a predetermined price at a specified time in the future. Futures contracts are traded on exchanges and are used for hedging risk or for speculative purposes.

Monetary Policy:

The process by which a central bank controls the supply of money, often targeting an inflation rate or interest rate to ensure economic stability and growth.

Inflation Targeting:

A monetary policy where the central bank sets a specific inflation rate as its goal. This approach aims to keep inflation within a targeted range to ensure economic stability.

Stagflation:

An economic condition characterized by slow growth, high unemployment, and rising prices (inflation).

Deflation:

A decrease in the general price level of goods and services. Deflation increases the real value of money over time, but can lead to decreased consumer spending and economic stagnation.

Hyperinflation:

An extremely high and typically accelerating rate of inflation, often exceeding 50% per month. Hyperinflation erodes the real value of the local currency, as the prices of all goods increase.

Open Market Operations (OMO):

Activities by a central bank to buy or sell government bonds on the open market to control the money supply and influence interest rates.

Yield Curve:

A graph that shows the relationship between interest rates and the maturity dates of debt securities. A normal yield curve slopes upward, indicating that longer-term debt securities have higher yields than short-term securities.

Liquidity:

Liquidity refers to how quickly and easily an asset can be converted into cash without significantly affecting its price. In financial markets, high liquidity means assets can be bought or sold quickly and with minimal price fluctuations.

Liquidity Trap:

A situation in which monetary policy becomes ineffective because the nominal interest rate is at or near zero, causing people to hoard cash rather than invest it, regardless of the amount of money the central bank injects into the economy.

Interest Rate Corridor:

The range between the central bank's lending rate and the deposit rate. The corridor helps manage liquidity in the banking system by setting the upper and lower bounds for short-term interest rates.

Phillips Curve:

An economic concept that shows an inverse relationship between the rate of unemployment and the rate of inflation in an economy. The Phillips Curve has been re-evaluated in recent years as its predictive power has weakened, and many central banks now rely on a broader range of indicators.

Fiscal Policy:

Government decisions about spending and taxation that impact the economy. Unlike monetary policy, which is implemented by central banks, fiscal policy is determined by the legislative and executive branches of government.

Capital Adequacy Ratio (CAR):

A measure of a bank's capital, expressed as a percentage of its risk-weighted credit exposures. It is used to protect depositors and promote the stability and efficiency of financial systems.

Basel III:

An international regulatory framework developed by the Basel Committee on Banking Supervision to strengthen regulation, supervision, and risk management within the banking sector.

Bailout:

Financial support to a company or country which faces serious financial difficulty or bankruptcy. The support can come in the form of loans, bonds, stocks, or cash.

Bail-In:

A mechanism in which a bank's creditors are required to bear some of the burden by having a portion of their debt written off or converted into equity to recapitalize the bank in distress.

Fractional Reserve Banking:

A banking system in which only a fraction of bank deposits are backed by actual cash on hand and are available for withdrawal. Banks lend out the majority of deposits to generate interest.

Credit Default Swap (CDS):

A financial derivative or contract that allows an investor to "swap" or offset their credit risk with that of another investor. For example, if a lender is worried that a borrower might default on a loan, they could use a CDS to transfer the risk.

Collateralized Debt Obligation (CDO):

A type of structured asset-backed security (ABS). A CDO is a pool of loans and other assets sold to institutional investors. The pooled assets are essentially debt obligations that serve as collateral for the CDO.

Mortgage-Backed Securities (MBS):

Investments that are secured by mortgages. An MBS is a type of asset-backed security that is secured by a collection of mortgages bought from the banks that issued them.

Stress Test:

An analysis or simulation designed to determine the ability of a financial institution to deal with an economic crisis. These tests are conducted by banks and regulators to ensure that the banks have enough capital to manage through difficult economic periods.

Liquidity Coverage Ratio (LCR):

A standard established by Basel III that aims to ensure that a financial institution has enough liquid assets to cover its cash outflows for 30 days during a financial stress scenario.

Net Stable Funding Ratio (NSFR):

Another Basel III standard that requires banks to maintain a stable funding profile in relation to their on- and off-balance sheet activities.

Systemically Important Financial Institution (SIFI):

A bank, insurance company, or other financial institution whose failure might trigger a financial crisis.

Macroprudential Policy:

A type of policy that focuses on reducing risk in the financial system as a whole, rather than regulating Individual financial institutions.

Microprudential Policy:

Policies and regulations designed to ensure the soundness of individual financial institutions, such as banks and insurance companies.

Hawkish:

A term used to describe central bank policies that are focused on controlling inflation and are likely to lead to higher interest rates.

Dovish:

A term used to describe central bank policies that are focused on stimulating economic growth and employment, typically involving lower interest rates.

Foreign Currency Reserves:

Holdings of foreign currencies by a central bank, used to back liabilities and influence monetary policy. These reserves are used to maintain the value of the national currency and ensure liquidity in times of financial instability.

Real GDP:

The total value of all goods and services produced in a country, adjusted for inflation. It provides a more accurate picture of an economy's size and growth over time, accounting for price changes.

Nominal GDP:

The total value of all goods and services produced in a country measured at current prices, without adjusting for inflation. It can be misleading when comparing growth over time because it does not account for changes in price levels.

Consumer Price Index (CPI):

A measure that examines the average change over time in the prices paid by consumers for a basket of goods and services. It's used as a key indicator of inflation. The CPI is calculated by tracking price changes for each item in a fixed basket of goods and services and averaging them, weighted by their relative importance.

Retail Price Index (RPI):

A measure of inflation that includes the cost of housing, such as mortgage interest payments, which makes it different from the CPI. It tracks the change in the price of a basket of goods and services over time and is often higher than CPI due to these additional costs.

Producer Price Index (PPI):

A measure of the average change over time in the selling prices received by domestic producers for their output. It is a leading indicator of consumer price inflation, as it measures price changes from the perspective of the seller.

Purchasing Managers' Index (PMI):

An indicator of the economic health of the manufacturing and service sectors, based on surveys of private-sector companies. It covers new orders, inventory levels, production, supplier deliveries, and employment conditions.

Balance of Trade:

The difference between a country's exports and imports. A surplus means a country exports more than it imports, while a deficit means it imports more than it exports. A trade surplus or deficit can have significant implications for a nation's economy and currency. For instance, a surplus might indicate strong production, but if it's due to weak domestic demand, it might also signal economic issues.

Money Supply (M0, M1, M2, M4):

These are different measures of the money supply in an economy:

- M0: The total of all physical currency (coins and notes) in circulation and deposits held by the central bank.
- M1: Includes M0 plus demand deposits, such as checking accounts.
- M2: Includes M1 plus savings accounts, small time deposits, and money market mutual funds.
- M4: Includes M3 (which encompasses larger time deposits, institutional money market funds, and other large liquid assets) and broad money, including deposits in the banking system.

Claimant Count Rate:

A measure of the number of people claiming unemployment benefits, providing an immediate snapshot of labour market conditions. It is calculated by tallying the total number of claimants each month.

ILO Unemployment Rate:

The International Labour Organization (ILO) Unemployment Rate measures the percentage of the labour force that is unemployed but actively seeking employment. It is based on the ILO's definition, which is widely used to ensure comparability across different countries. The ILO is a United Nations agency that sets international labour standards and promotes social justice and fair work conditions worldwide.

House Price Index:

A measure that tracks changes in the price of residential properties, reflecting the health of the housing market and consumer wealth. It's calculated by comparing current prices of sold houses to previous periods.

Mortgage Approvals:

Indicates the number of mortgages approved for house purchases, signalling future housing market activity and consumer confidence. Calculated by tracking the volume of mortgage loan approvals each month.

Public Sector Net Borrowing (PSNB):

A measure of the difference between government spending and revenue, highlighting the government's fiscal position and public sector financial health. Calculated by subtracting total government revenues from total government expenditures.

Debt-to-GDP Ratio:

A measure of a country's national debt compared to its GDP, indicating the country's ability to pay back its debt. A high ratio can signal economic risk.

Inflation Expectations:

Predictions of future inflation rates, which influence consumer behaviour and wage negotiations. Measured through surveys and market-based indicators like inflation-protected securities.

Business Inventories:

The amount of goods that businesses have in stock, indicating future production activity. Low inventories may lead to increased production.

Exchange Rates:

The value of a country's currency compared to another currency, affecting trade balances and economic stability. Exchange rates are determined by the foreign exchange market.

Commodity Prices:

The prices of essential goods like oil, gold, and agricultural products, which affect inflation and the cost of goods. These prices are tracked by commodity exchanges.

Budget Deficit/Surplus:

The difference between what the government spends and what it earns in revenue (taxes, fees, etc.). A deficit occurs when spending exceeds revenue, and a surplus occurs when revenue exceeds spending.

Savings Rate:

The portion of income that households save rather than spend. It indicates future spending capacity and financial health.

Corporate Profits:

The earnings of companies, which indicate business health and can lead to increased investment and hiring.

Productivity:

The output per worker or per hour worked. Higher productivity means more efficient production and economic growth. It is calculated using data on output and hours worked.

Capacity Utilization:

A measure of how much of a country's production capacity is being used. It indicates the level of demand and potential inflationary pressures.

Real Effective Exchange Rate (REER):

A weighted average of a country's currency relative to a basket of other major currencies, adjusted for inflation. It indicates the relative value of the currency in the context of international trade.

Phillips Curve:

An economic concept that suggests an inverse relationship between unemployment and inflation. However, this relationship has been less reliable in recent decades, leading many economists to question its predictive power. Many central banks now use a broader range of indicators to guide monetary policy decisions.

Labour Force Participation Rate:

The percentage of the working-age population that is either employed or actively seeking employment. It is an indicator of overall economic activity.

Net Trade Balance:

The difference between a country's total exports and imports. A positive balance indicates a trade surplus, while a negative balance indicates a trade deficit.

Money Market Rate:

The interest rate on short-term loans between banks or other financial institutions. It is a key indicator of short-term liquidity in the financial system.

Sectoral Balances:

The financial balances of different sectors of the economy, such as households, businesses, and the government. Understanding these balances can help in assessing economic sustainability.

MPC Minutes:

Minutes from the Monetary Policy Committee meetings, where interest rate decisions are made. These minutes provide insight into the committee's deliberations and future policy direction.

Current Account Balance:

The difference between a nation's savings and its investment. It includes trade balance, net income from abroad, and net current transfers. A surplus indicates the nation is a net lender, while a deficit indicates it is a net borrower.

Gilt Yields:

The return on UK government bonds (gilts). Gilt yields are an important indicator of investor confidence and the cost of government borrowing.

M0, M1, M2, M3:

These are different measures of the money supply:

- M0: The total of all physical currency in circulation.
- M1: M0 plus demand deposits.
- M2: M1 plus savings deposits, small time deposits, and money market funds.
- M3: M2 plus large time deposits and institutional money market funds.

Initial Margin:

Initial Margin is the amount of capital required to open a position in a financial market. It acts as a security deposit that ensures the buyer or seller can meet their financial obligations.

Variation Margin:

Variation Margin refers to the additional funds that must be deposited by an investor to cover any losses as market conditions fluctuate. It ensures that the margin account remains funded to cover potential losses.

Collateral:

Collateral is an asset that a borrower offers to a lender to secure a loan. If the borrower fails to repay the loan, the lender can seize the collateral to recover their losses. Common types of collateral include property, stocks, and bonds.

Trading:

Trading involves buying and selling financial assets such as stocks, bonds, commodities, or currencies. Trading can occur on exchanges or over-the-counter markets, with the goal of making a profit from price changes.

Equity:

Equity represents ownership in a company. It is the value of shares issued by a company, giving shareholders a claim on the company's assets and profits. In finance, equity is often associated with stock ownership.

Fixed Income:

Fixed Income refers to investments that provide regular, fixed returns, such as bonds. These investments typically pay interest at regular intervals and return the principal amount at maturity.

Capital Requirement:

Capital Requirement is the minimum amount of capital a bank or financial institution must hold as required by financial regulators. This is to ensure that the institution can absorb losses and remain solvent in times of financial stress.

Risk-Weighted Assets (RWA):

Risk-Weighted Assets (RWA) are used to determine the minimum amount of capital that a bank must hold to reduce the risk of insolvency. Assets are weighted according to their risk, with higher-risk assets requiring more capital to cover potential losses.

Reserve Requirement:

Reserve Requirement is the minimum amount of reserves (cash or deposits) that a bank must hold, either in its vaults or with the central bank. This is used to control the money supply and ensure the bank's liquidity.

References

Combined References

1. Federal Reserve. (2020). *What is the federal funds rate and how is it used in monetary policy?* Retrieved from Federal Reserve Education (https://www.federalreserveeducation.org/).

2. Federal Reserve. (2021). Monetary Policy Report. Retrieved from Federal Reserve.

3. European Central Bank. (2021). Repo operations. Retrieved from ECB Website (https://www.ecb.europa.eu/).

4. European Central Bank. (2020). *Monetary Policy Decisions*. Retrieved from ECB Publications (https://www.ecb.europa.eu/pub/html/index.en.html).

5. Financial Stability Board. (2014). *Reforming Major Interest Rate Benchmarks.* Retrieved from FSB Website (https://www.fsb.org/).

6. Financial Stability Board. (2019). *FSB Reports on Implementation of G20 Financial Reforms.* Retrieved from FSB Reports (https://www.fsb.org/).

7. Bank for International Settlements. (2020). *Capital Requirements.* Retrieved from BIS Website (https://www.bis.org/).

8. Bank for International Settlements. (2019). *Annual Economic Report.* Retrieved from BIS Publications.

9. Bank of England. (2024). Bank of England Quarterly Bulletin. Retrieved from BoE Website (https://www.bankofengland.co.uk/).

10. International Monetary Fund. (2023). *World Economic Outlook Report* Retrieved from IMF Website (https://www.imf.org/).

11. Office for National Statistics. (2024). *UK Economic Indicators Report.* Retrieved from ONS Website (https://www.ons.gov.uk/).

12. Federal Reserve Education. (2024). *Monetary Policy Tools Explained.* Retrieved from Federal Reserve Education (https://www.federalreserveeducation.org/).

www.ingramcontent.com/pod-product-compliance
Ingram Content Group UK Ltd.
Pitfield, Milton Keynes, MK11 3LW, UK
UKHW062255290726
14090UKWH00017B/705

9 781068 553004